Missing
In
Action

Missing In Action

How Mothers Lose, Grieve, and Retrieve Their Sense of Self

Anne M. Smollon, MSW

iUniverse, Inc.

New York Lincoln Shanghai

Missing In Action
How Mothers Lose, Grieve, and Retrieve Their Sense of Self

iUniverse books may be ordered through booksellers or by contacting:

iUniverse
2021 Pine Lake Road, Suite 100
Lincoln, NE 68512
www.iuniverse.com
1-800-Authors (1-800-288-4677)

The information, ideas, and suggestions in this book are not intended as a substitute for professional medical advice. Before following any suggestions contained in this book, consult your physician. Neither the author nor the publisher shall be liable or responsible for any loss or damage allegedly arising as a consequence of your use or application of any information or suggestions in this book.

ISBN: 978-0-595-41324-9 (pbk)
ISBN: 978-0-595-85677-0 (ebk)

Printed in the United States of America

For my mother, Rita Sakowicz,
and the children who made me the mother I am today

CONTENTS

Prologue 1

Introduction 3

One: The Metamorphosis 7

Two: What's There to Lose? 25

Three: About Grief 39

Four: Maternal Intrapersonal ANXIETY: Why Anxiety and Where It
    Begins 58

Five: The Ripple Effect 70

Six: The Boundary Hunter 79

Seven: Grief in Action 89

Eight: Through the Eyes of Love: The Final Goals 100

A Tribute 113

References 115

ACKNOWLEDGMENTS

This book would not be what it is without all the mothers who contributed their unthinkable thoughts, difficult feelings, stories, feedback, and encouragement. Thank you for holding me accountable to produce a text that will help other mothers. I wish to thank neighbors for their heartfelt support and friends who read each draft with great care and love, especially Danya Kane, my dearest friend; she redefined my concept of friendship. To Irena Sikorova, a wonderful young lady who entered my life at the most perfect time. She took over many of my tasks so that I could rejuvenate, think, and write. She worked hard to give me and my children what we needed. I thank her from the bottom of my heart. I also need to thank Dr. Shari Munch, who heard my idea for a book three years ago and encouraged me throughout its development with much enthusiasm, advice, and professional input. Her feedback was invaluable to me as I aspired to convey my thoughts in the most precise way. Allison Hargraves utilized her keen eye and professional skills to edit my final draft. I appreciate her time, effort, and unwitting "push" to get this book off my desk. To my brother Bill Sakowicz, who babysat, made meals, ran errands, and listened when I anxiously and neurotically needed to vent. There is no better brother, uncle, or friend. To my family, especially my parents, Rita and John Sakowicz, who cheered me along every step I took on the rutted road of creativity and motherhood. They always believed a book was in me, and they were right. Thank you for all your love, your faith in me, and your devotion to my well-being. A special thanks to my dad for designing the perfect book cover and to Jesse Rinyu, who generated the computer image that gave life to my father's design. I also must thank my children, Leigh Ann, Laura, and Daniel. Leigh Ann is the light of my life, Laura my hero and heartbeat, and Daniel is literally the dream that came true, but better. They are indeed the best part of me. Thank you for understanding all the times I put you off so that I could pursue my work as a writer and a mental health professional on a mission. Finally, I need to thank my husband, Jim, despite the lack of words to convey my gratitude, love, and admiration. He cast light on many dark moments with his gentle touch, sense of humor, and loving gaze. He has been my backbone, my sounding board, my coach, and perhaps my biggest fan. I certainly know that I am his. Thank you for getting me through a tough chapter of my life by knowing what I had forgotten.

A.M.S.

PROLOGUE

Leigh Ann came quietly. My husband, Jim, was the first to touch her as she arrived fully into our world. He literally glowed as he laid Leigh Ann in my arms, this small creature with lots of dark hair and big eyes that were already fixed on mine. We held our baby close and said nothing for a long time as though our feelings escaped any attempt we could ever make to express them in words. It was one of those rare moments in my life when I would have gladly stopped time and stayed forever. What a sense of relief and joy to see the baby that had kept me company for almost a year. But in what seemed to be the very next moment my world did stop, but not for me to enjoy. It's hard for me to think about, let alone write about, the memory of Leigh Ann's seizures and the doctor who described all the possible reasons for them. I learned the true meaning of inconsolable that day, especially as the doctor took Leigh Ann from my arms and told me that I would not be taking her home as I had planned. Instead she would be taken to the Neonatal Intensive Care Unit (NICU) for diagnostic procedures and medical interventions. Jim followed, determined to stay close to the little girl who had instantly become the center of our universe. I stayed behind and cried in my room for hours, waiting for any news Jim might bring. Eventually he came back, looking pale but composed, obviously worn down by the events unfolding in the NICU. I could tell he was trying his best to keep me calm, but the words "brain hemorrhage" have a way of inflicting terror despite the gentle tone in which they are spoken.

Leigh Ann remained in the NICU for a full week obtaining the care she needed for a brain hemorrhage that had spontaneously occurred during her birth. But by week's end we were home with our daughter and ready for the life we had imagined apart from the regimen of medications that had to be administered in the right amounts at the right times. Unfortunately, though, things didn't go quite as we anticipated. Leigh Ann had a few setbacks that prevented her from keeping food (and medicine) down. She was described as "failing to thrive" somewhere in her third month, which landed her in The Children's Hospital of Philadelphia. After days of examinations and tests, we left Philadelphia with Leigh Ann, once again en route toward the life we had dreamed of having with our baby. This time the dream was fulfilled.

Leigh Ann made a full recovery and was as precious a baby as babies come. She filled our lives with gratitude, wonder, and extraordinary love as she evolved from baby to active toddler. Jim had long since returned to work and Leigh Ann and I went about our lives discovering every back road, park, and activity designed for children. We passed the days with books, chores, and every neighborhood toddler with mom in tow. From the outside life looked great, but slowly and unimaginably the dream of living happily with a healthy baby faded as reality took hold: Life with a toddler is demanding. The dream I had once envisioned never included the physical care, housekeeping, patience, chores, sacrifice, mental focus, and discipline a child needs on a daily basis. The dream left out how my friendships would wane and my self-esteem would falter. For this, and so much more, I was not prepared. Nor was I prepared for the onslaught of conflicting feelings and angst that grew greater, though intermittently, with each day I spent at home with my daughter, and more noticeably in the years that followed when my family grew to include two more children, Laura and Daniel. I was overwhelmed with work and frozen in a place that excluded *me*. In an indeterminable moment I must have let go of my "self" to fully assume the role of mother and all that it entails. However, for years I grieved the sense of self that I lost. I grieved deeply, unsuspectingly, and alone.

INTRODUCTION

Most of us associate grief with the death of a loved one. Understandably, this kind of loss is our greatest cause for grief. Yet grief may exist during other occasions, even occasions that accent our lives in positive ways. That's because change naturally engenders elements of both loss and gain. Whereas one might gain a tremendous amount from a particular life-changing event, he or she must simultaneously let go of what previously had been, which could incite grief for various reasons. Becoming a mother is one such major life-changing event. It's a time full of indescribable pleasures that have intoxicated generations of mothers past and present. However, for many women there is a darker side to motherhood; it's a side that weeps, despairs, and yearns in moments weaved throughout the exhilaration. Through countless conversations and structured interviews, I've discovered that these moments cause mothers to grieve. They grieve over such things as the loss of former friendships, physique, income, independence, and self-esteem. Perhaps in the most profound way, women often grieve the loss of spousal intimacy and the loss that occurs when their sense of self deteriorates in all the work, details, and changes associated with motherhood. When mothers lose their sense of self, they often exhibit the physical, emotional, cognitive, and behavioral symptoms that are typically ascribed to grief. And why shouldn't they grieve? Grieving is the natural response to losing something of value. The problem is, our society doesn't recognize this kind of loss for mothers or acknowledge the grief it causes them to experience. This indifference often causes the grief to manifest in any one of many unhealthy ways for women and their families.

Motherhood is one of the biggest, if not *the* biggest, transitional period of a woman's life, and yet we as a society trust that all is well despite the signs and symptoms of distress that mothers often exhibit in the first few years of motherhood. As a mother and a mental health professional, I could no longer turn a blind eye. Maternal Intrapersonal Anxiety (MIA) is a term I have coined to characterize the grief I believe mothers experience when they lose their sense of self. It's a grief that is generally obscured by the happy nature of childbirth, the many needs of young children, the better moments, society's unrealistic expectations of mothers, and the fear of rejection and sense of shame that surrounds a woman's conflicting feelings. These reasons aside, grief exists and generates MIA. MIA is the manifestation of unrecognized and unacknowledged grief. Maternal, of course, identifies mothers. Intrapersonal simply means *within* the person rather than between persons as in the word interpersonal. In MIA mothers experience the loss of a pre-child identity (and the aspects of their lives associated with that identity); it's an internal processing of change, an internal experience that perceives a familiar image lost as the demands, sacrifices, and responsibilities of motherhood expand. It does not in any way involve the loss of a significant other person.

The word "anxiety" in the term Maternal Intrapersonal Anxiety represents the core experience of grief. This anxiety is intended to highlight the relation between the many symptoms mothers experience and grief as understood in a grief theory known as *Grief as a function of Separation Anxiety* set forth by David Switzer, a pastoral theologian. This theory maintains that anxiety is the underlying emotion in grief. Symptoms of grief (e.g., fatigue, anger, guilt, depression, social withdrawal) are not separate from this anxiety, but rather relate directly to it. From Switzer's perspective, anxiety exists at a primal level and is evoked when something of value is lost. Losing a valued person, image, idea, object, place, or construct (e.g., sense of self) can all elicit grief, which is central in MIA.

MIA is not related to Postpartum Depression (PPD), a condition that occurs during childbirth or the period immediately following the birth of a baby. The symptoms of PPD include depression, guilt, and anxiety; however, doctors suspect that the hormonal fluctuations that follow a birth contribute largely to the symptoms that new mothers experience during this time, and the symptoms usually subside within eighteen months. In contrast, MIA is not hormonally driven and it does not subside within eighteen months. In fact, MIA may evidence in pregnancy and in the first year of motherhood, but it usually surges **after** the eighteen-month "honeymoon period" and continues in the years that follow when mothers are inundated with the enormous and all-consuming challenges that their children pose. These challenges typically leave little time or energy for mothers to care for the self within them that gives shape to any identity apart from that of mother. That is, mothers rarely nurture the elements of their lives that function to maintain the healthy personal boundaries essential to a healthy sense of self.

Keeping healthy boundaries is a difficult task at best for most mothers. However, not all mothers experience the loss of self and the ensuing grief that I describe in this book. That is, some mothers may *miss* certain aspects of their pre-child identity, but they may not perceive change as loss and will therefore not grieve. Other mothers will see themselves repeatedly throughout the pages of this book. The material is strictly my perspective as a social worker, an NLP (Neuro-Linguistic Programming) practitioner, and a happily married, Caucasian middle-class woman in her forties with three children under the age of ten who has experienced this kind of grief firsthand. This is my reference point. I don't know how far my assertions extend beyond this point except for the feedback and stories I recorded from so many mothers. I interviewed mothers with diverse circumstances and various backgrounds, mothers from different ethnic groups and economic levels to provide data from as broad a spectrum as possible. However, the majority of my interviews were with stay-at-home mothers of young children, and I focused on material related to MIA.

MIA is a condition worth observing and discussing, despite the controversy it may elicit. Too many mothers are out there struggling with feelings and symptoms they don't understand. Mothers know that they feel depressed, anxious, or tired. They know that they are often short-tempered and irritable. They know that something is not right, but they cannot pinpoint the reason as easily as they can articulate their feelings or list their symptoms. Typically mothers just think they are drained by the responsibilities that are innate to motherhood. However true this might be, it doesn't explain the *depth* and *intensity* of the feelings and symptoms they relate in private. In other words, something more is going on. I propose that the greater, deeper experience of angst that mothers know may have its origin in the lost sense of self that they rarely discuss, recognize, or understand.

The Motherhood Report: How Women Feel about Being Mothers, published in 1987, was one of the first books to cite the experience of childbirth on mothers, including stress, myths related to motherhood, anger, the mother-child connection, and the ambivalence and growth inherent in the role of mother. In 1999 author Susan Maushart did a fine job exposing the conspiracy of silence mothers maintain about their mixed emotions in her book *The Mask of Motherhood,* as did other authors with a similar agenda. Books about personal experiences and reflections on motherhood also exist. From a more political perspective, we have books such as *The Price of Motherhood: Why the Most Important Job in the World Is Still the Least Valued,* published in 2001, *The Mommy Myth,* published in 2004, and more recently, *Perfect Madness: Motherhood in the Age of Anxiety.*

Apart from books on mothers and motherhood, there are so many more books addressing grief, grief of all kinds and from nearly every perspective. Among all these books I did expect motherhood to be mentioned (even if occasionally) as an example of a transitional period that may cause women to experience aspects of loss and grief, but I have yet to see this. Interestingly, in *Perfect Madness: Motherhood in the Age of Anxiety,* author Judith Warner writes, "The feeling has many faces, but it doesn't really have a name." I think it does. It's called grief, and I felt it was time to tell mothers, "It's okay to grieve. Your life has changed in many ways since you've become a mother, and it's reasonable to grieve if any of those changes adversely affected some area of your life or your sense of self, even if only temporarily. Thoughts and feelings related to grief do not reflect on you as a bad mother, a bad person, or a person who is unable or unfit for parenting." *Missing In Action: How Mothers Lose, Grieve, and Retrieve Their Sense of Self* says this and much more.

Throughout *Missing In Action: How Mothers Lose, Grieve, and Retrieve Their Sense of Self,* I use research, personal experience, and stories told by other mothers to make my assertions cogent. I begin by illustrating the numerous changes that occur for women once they become mothers and discuss how differently women perceive those changes. Then I describe six distinct categories of loss and demonstrate how mothers encounter them, often simultaneously, in the early years of motherhood. I illuminate the compelling similarities between what many mothers describe (socially, emotionally, behaviorally, and cognitively) and the characteristics of grief, responses to grief, and symptoms related to grief. Chapter 4 clarifies what MIA is and how it results when personal boundaries deteriorate; I also refine the concept of personal boundaries, how they are violated, and why they must be preserved. In Chapter 5, I indulge my desire to explain how mood and behavior get passed along among family members before I address the value of a healthy sense of self and how mothers can create the appropriate boundaries that secure that sense of self.

The final chapters address goals that serve to reclaim a sense of self gone astray. I elaborate on each goal, particularly the last two, which focus on the process of relearning the world and oneself in a world forever altered by the children who enter it. Each goal is a step that leads to a life beyond the distress that often accompanies motherhood. By providing personal experience and stories of other mothers, my ultimate hope is to instill a sense of camaraderie in all the mothers who read this book. The stories are intended to help mothers feel less alone, to validate their feelings and concerns, and to offer hope that they will evolve into the mothers and women they aspire to become as the transition period fades.

Anne M. Smollon, MSW
January 2006

ONE:
THE METAMORPHOSIS

○ ○

"Drastic change creates an estrangement from the self, and generates a need for a new birth of a new identity. And it perhaps depends on the way this need is satisfied whether the process of change runs smoothly or is attended with convulsions and explosions."

—*Eric Hoffer,* **The Temper of Our Time**

For many women the challenge to adjust to motherhood moves at a pace and strength that is greater than they expected. A tidal wave moving swiftly toward an unsuspecting beach dweller is the image that comes to mind. At least that's how it felt to me. Like I was hit by a tidal wave and I was drowning in water that was too deep and too rough for this average swimmer. The simple truth is that life changes with a child, as does a woman. Eight years ago I foolishly thought that only my life circumstances would change after I had a baby. I knew there would be lots of dirty diapers and toys scattered around every room in the house. I figured that I would be hanging around playgrounds more often than the local café with friends and traveling less spontaneously and more with port-a-cribs, bottles, and booster seats. I don't know, maybe I wasn't nearly as ready for motherhood as I thought at the time I conceived. I didn't realize how much sacrifice was involved or how little I knew about coping. I figured I was mature and in a happy relationship and therefore I would transition well, but I didn't. In fact, I struggled with "convulsions and explosions," as Hoffer would say, and shed lots of tears. Obviously, the process of change did not run smoothly for me.

Perhaps I made a big mistake by anticipating the "hardest job in the world" by only visualizing the physical nature of childcare, not by preparing for the effect motherhood would have on me psychologically, spiritually, emotionally, mentally, socially, cognitively, behaviorally, sexually, and financially. On the other hand, how does one prepare for such wide-ranging effects? The changes can be lurking in the subtle decline of intimacy between partners or as brazen as weight gain. For me it started innocently with clothes that were less about style and more about their ability to withstand the abuse of dirty hands and spit-up, and a haircut that was more convenient than attractive. I have the pictures if you need the proof. There were other changes in my physical appearance, but those changes were of a much more intimate kind. Let's just say that I am no longer perky and leave it at that. More disturbing, however, were the changes in my state of mind. There were myriad states of mind ranging from the ecstasy of just giving birth to the fury that arises when parent needs collide with toddler needs. Those were the obvious, and momentary, states of mind.

Far more penetrating were the insidious changes in my mood, which moved along steadily and consistently toward discontent. My days were filling with a growing sense of restlessness and depression. I couldn't quite figure out what was wrong with me. I had beautiful and healthy children. I was thrilled that they had each other. I thought I had what I wanted. And yet I was so unhappy. This unhappiness was making it hard for me to get through each day. Now, granted, my days were full of doing laundry, dishes, food shopping, vacuuming, changing diapers, cooking, cleaning, and taking care of the numerous needs of three young children. Few people could get through a day like that with a smile on their face. On the other hand, I was becoming more aware of the adverse changes in my disposition and the things I told myself. In fact, my words took on the voice of a character I referred to as the Mother Maid. She kept me company as I complained through each endless chore and every obligation. I mumbled in her voice as I started each day aware of the responsibilities I knew were mine, responsibilities I began to describe as mindless, unsatisfying, and downright dreadful.

The Mother Maid was a disgruntled mom for sure, overworked and overwhelmed, with a bitter voice that was hard to hear, even for me. Sadly, I knew I was actually becoming the Mother Maid. What I didn't realize, however, was how much I missed the person that my new role as mother had claimed. My feelings had cleverly worked themselves into my life disguised as the depression, angst, resentment, frustration, anger, fatigue, and martyrdom that might accompany the hard and consistent labor of motherhood. Unfortunately, though, these feelings played a kind of tug-of-war with my desire to be the best parent I could be for my children. That is, I wanted to do right by my children, but it was getting increasingly more difficult to fight the force working against me. Regrettably for my family and me, I didn't recognize my feelings for what they really were. I just knew that I was unhappy.

Apart from being unhappy, I had also become many other things that I didn't like. Mostly, I had become impatient and serious. I lost my sense of humor. When you lose your sense of humor, especially as a parent, life can, and usually does, take on a completely different view. Similarly, I suppose, when you lose your patience. I also noticed that I had trouble concentrating, which other mothers told me happened because "having young children does that to a mother." I did have some good days, but the bad days became more frequent. My husband urged me to find babysitters and outside help, as though it was my sole responsibility to do so, but I couldn't. As much as I agreed with him that I could use the respite, something beyond me prevented me from making the necessary effort. I felt paralyzed to act on my own behalf, which was hard to explain and understand. My husband became as frustrated with me as I was with myself for not getting the support that was certain to make a difference in my life. Because I never reached out for help, I felt as though I lost the "right" to complain, which made things even worse. I eventually turned inward, withdrew from family and friends, and rarely talked about the pain I was feeling, although I am sure it was apparent to anyone who knew me well.

The pivotal moment came when I realized that I didn't like myself. I had changed, but not in the ways that I wanted for myself. I didn't like the person I was becoming, and I was blaming it on my life that had changed. Because the link between having children and my life changing seemed so obvious, I understand how I could have looked upon my children as the reason for my unhappiness. They weren't. In fact, it was only after I acknowledged this fact that I more closely examined my life and the way I had been feeling. Being a social worker, I knew I had to take a step back and, with a therapist's perspective, look at my "symptoms." Much to my surprise, I discovered that my symptoms resembled those related to grief. Because I had experienced the loss of several family members over the years and I had worked for hospice as a grief counselor, I knew the symptoms of grief. It just never occurred to me that I was grieving. I was grieving because I *had* lost someone—me! I had taken on the role of mother in a single instant and became so completely immersed in the lives of my children and the house in which they lived. Through the years of caring for them and neglecting myself, I became estranged from the person that I had been for the three decades prior to having children. I lost touch with almost everything about me that I once valued and considered familiar. In short, the "old" me was gone.

From the many interviews I conducted, I learned that I was not alone in my experience. Most women undergo and acknowledge a drastic change in their sense of identity, thinking of themselves first as mothers and second as wives, daughters, sisters, and friends, respectively. Second to identity these women confessed that their self-image declined after they had a baby. They felt less attractive and more "frumpy." They rarely looked good leaving the house during the day and were even less appealing getting into bed at night. Sex appeal was no longer held up as an aspiration but more as a construct intended to shame them. In addition, a large number of mothers described the mental, psychological, and financial adjustment from a life of status in the workforce to a life of routine at home with a purple dinosaur named Barney and Muppets of different shapes and colors that came to visit each and every morning. Other telling feedback included how relationships, priorities, dress sizes, responsibilities, eating and sleeping habits, goals, cognitive skills, and general dispositions changed unexpectedly, and sometimes quite radically, as the result of becoming mothers.

Cari shares her experience:

I don't know how it happened or why, for that matter, but things changed. I changed. Honestly, I felt a heightened awareness for all the things that could happen to my baby. I think that is what started my obsessive behaviors. Never before had I been this compulsive type person, and yet here I was yanking door handles almost until they broke, just to be certain that they were locked. Before I knew it, I was this nervous type, always expecting that something bad would happen if I relaxed. Even long after the baby grew older, I was consistently hyper about things, most things. I didn't want to be like this. I took meds to help, but I knew it wasn't a chemical thing. I just wanted to feel like the old me. The old me was confident and unshaken by things; I was a businesswoman who had her life together and her head together. It's really weird what happened. My family tells me to "just stop," like stop worrying and stop checking on my daughter, but it's just not as easy as it sounds.

Lauren B.

Well, of course I noticed instantly how my body changed. I didn't like the changes, but I figured it was normal. Once I was done nursing, I thought I would get back my shape, but it wasn't as easy as that. My breasts never looked the same, nor did my hips, for that matter. [She smirks.] I still have my baby weight, which I assume I will keep until I can exercise more regularly. But I do not have the body I had before Dillon came along. No way.

Connie

Oh, so much has changed. Where do I begin? I guess what I miss the most is my sense of financial independence. I seem to never have money on me. I always have to ask my husband for money. That feels bad to me. Imagine. I ask him for money in order to buy him birthday presents or an anniversary gift. Very weird for me. I used to always have my own bank account and earnings. I used to make good money, actually. So to go from a good income to no income was radical for me. I hate feeling so dependent on someone else, even for the smallest things.

Lynn M.

Of all the things that changed, I think the worst was the changes in my mood. I became so moody. [She laughs.] *By moody, I guess I mean cranky. I'm cranky a lot. I guess because I'm always so tired. I've got three young and active kids. I hop from one thing to the next, from one kid to the next. I'm tired, really tired. And I'm cranky. It's hard to manage the temper tantrums and all the needs and not be cranky. My husband couldn't do it. He wouldn't even try. So when I get cranky, he just backs off. I wish he would take the kids when he backs off, but like I said, he just can't be with them for too long.*

Lorraine

How have I changed? Oh my God. How have I changed? How has my life changed? Oh jeez. [She shakes her head back and forth.] *No one ever asked me to answer such a question. Let's see. How have I changed? You know, the question arouses such feelings. It's like I never thought about it, but I live it daily. I know I've changed so much, and yet I don't think about it. And now, thinking about it, I feel overwhelmed.* [She pauses for a long while.] *My marriage changed. It might not be the biggest change, but it's the change that I hate the most.* [She says this as if asking a question.] *John and I were always so physical, holding hands, sitting next to each other. That kind of stuff. We just don't do that stuff anymore. I really miss it. I also need it. I feel like all of me gives attention to the kids and then I need a little something for myself, like attention, love. We've talked about it, and I know he means to be there for me, but things are just different. He's caught up in his own world trying to provide for us. We both have jobs to do, and we do them. I just wish we had a little something left over for each other.*

Janet

I know one way I've changed for sure. [She looks around her kitchen.] *I'm not nearly as neat, clean, or orderly as I used to be. I mean, look around. My floors were never this dirty, ever. I hate it, I really do, but I can't keep up. My whole house is filthy. I used to be embarrassed, but I don't entertain here anymore so ...* [She never finishes her sentence.]

I asked Janet if she used to entertain often and if she missed hosting events and parties in her home.

Janet

Oh my God, yes. Jack and I used to always have people over. His family, my family, our friends. We don't do it anymore. And yes, I really miss it. It's just too much work now. I can't imagine putting that element back in our lives, at least while the kids are young. There's really not too much adult time left in our lives. My day is full with the kids, and by the time I put them to bed, well, you know. I'm not going to be hosting any parties, that's for sure.

Gina

I know how my husband would answer that question. He'd say that we don't have anywhere near as much sex as we used to. I guess it's my fault. I don't want it like I used to. I'm too tired, and I'm not in the mood after a long day with the kids. And I can't believe that he would want to have sex with me. I think I look so unappealing. It's not like I'm getting into bed wearing some sexy little teddy or anything. Quite honestly, I think I look gross. I feel gross anyway.

Megan

You know, I was thinking about this the other day. I realized that I'm not ambitious anymore. I had plans for myself. A career track, things I wanted to accomplish. I haven't thought about my plans or goals for such a long time. I guess they don't mean as much to me anymore.

I asked Megan, "Is that all right with you? Often during the course of our lives, our priorities change, our plans change. We take on new goals. Is that how you see your life?"

Megan

Yes and no. Of course I've taken on new responsibilities, but I'd still like to do something for myself. Accomplish something I've set out to do that holds great interest for me. I love politics. I always thought I would be more politically active. I was going to finish my master's and see what opened up for me. I can't tell you now exactly what I would want to be doing, but I do miss the personal satisfaction I used to have working and going to school years ago.

Clearly, women experience all kinds of change once they become mothers; in fact *all* women experience change. Unfortunately, some women have a harder time adjusting to these changes than other women. When I think back over my first five years as a mother, I can hardly believe what a difficult time I had adjusting. It's hard to believe that I wore my hair as I did or chose the clothes that I wore. It's hard to believe that I lost interest in my favorite hobbies and neglected to see good friends. I can't believe that I gave up on my goal to be a writer and rarely had the desire to be intimate with my husband. I can't believe how I wished myself away as often as I did. And most especially, I can't believe that I ever had such conflicting feelings toward the children I adore or such angst in a role that brings great joy to my life. Prior to having children, no one could have described motherhood to me in a way that would have prepared me for what actually happened. That is, I could not have prepared for the drastic changes that coincided with motherhood. No woman can. Women who become mothers must adjust to changes most of them never saw coming. Some changes happen instantly after a baby while others evolve slowly and clandestinely. For instance, my free time certainly changed in a heartbeat, as did my income. But I didn't wake up one day without patience or my sense of humor; these slipped out of reach as I coped less efficiently with the challenges of homemaker and mother that grew steadily toward monumental. By the time Daniel was born, I was taking daily breakdown breaks (a.k.a. DBBs) in the attic and losing the battle to convince others that I was fine.

Life with children requires a 24/7 commitment, a commitment mothers are expected to meet with abundant tolerance, selflessness, and surreal endurance.

For example, I have attended numerous playdates and too many mom-and-tot events to mention. I answer an average of ninety questions a day per child, listen to every wonder a child can imagine, and sidestep, with uncanny strategy, many tantrums in the making. I've become a light sleeper so that I can hear my babies cry when they need me through the night. I have nursed in awkward places and have taken great care to ensure that my children know that Mommy is there for them. I have food for their bellies and the right clothes to keep them comfortable. I read to them and let them make some choices for themselves. I referee, discipline, sacrifice, arbitrate, negotiate, and apologize when I make mistakes. I create structure, safety, and opportunities for growth. In every action I take, I am aware that I am being watched by children who look to me for the most critical lessons in living life: the lessons to be patient, to share, and to not hurt your sister, your brother, or others; the lessons to forgive, to take turns, and to be safe; the lessons to focus, practice, and work hard; the lessons to be empathic, confident, kind, honest, and moral; the lessons to not overdo, to play fair, to be proud of themselves, and to let go when they are ready.

These are only a few of the many physical and mental "actions" involved in raising a child. Far less glamorous but equally taxing on a mother are the jobs *related* to the children. For example, I wash at least a load of laundry every couple of days. I shop for food, bring it home, and cook it. I cook again in the morning, and then clean the mess. I make lunch, and then clean the mess. And then, of course, it's time for dinner, and I cook again. After I clean up the dinner mess, I am inclined to tackle the mess that the children made while I was cooking. I ask my young crew to help clean the house in order to teach them about responsibility and order, but I know I'll be doing most of it after they are asleep. In the meantime, the house is noisy as the children plot activities to sabotage my efforts to prepare them for bed. I watch the clock as it ticks closer to the time when I can sit down *alone*. I finish up the night by reading to the children before putting them to bed, which takes the last of any energy I may have had for an activity that was reserved for me, like reading a novel or visiting with my husband. Instead, while I sit, I mentally review my checklist. Have I done everything that needed doing today? Is the homework finished? Did the children brush their teeth? Are the lunches packed for school? Did all the phone calls get returned? Did I turn on the dryer and start the dishwasher? How about the thank-you cards for the gifts given to my daughter for her birthday (because there is always something left to do)? I finally go to bed knowing that another day follows that will work me as hard as it has today. It will be another day with no time or energy to exercise or see a friend for lunch unless I arrange for a babysitter who is competent, reliable, and trustworthy. This, of course, requires research beyond my fully engaged schedule and existing level of burnout.

With all the work and sacrifices associated with motherhood, how could a woman not change? Change *is* inevitable. However, a woman's *perception of change* is what will inevitably determine whether her transition into motherhood "runs smoothly or is attended with convulsions and explosions."

Perception

My model of MIA begins with change but rests squarely on the concept of perception. Perception is how we experience or become aware of the world, and it is paramount in understanding why we think and act as we do. When we perceive our environment, we gather information from what we see, hear, touch, smell, and taste. This information gets transmitted to the brain via the nervous system. The brain then determines what we do with that information, keeping in mind that the brain often deletes, distorts, and generalizes much of the information it receives. Likewise, the brain processes most of the information it receives at a level beyond our conscious awareness or thought; that is, most of what we gather through our five senses is processed and translated at an unconscious level. As a result, we can be unaware of any beliefs (about ourselves and the world) and thinking patterns that become aberrant and/or automatic (e.g., "I can't do anything right"). With such thoughts limiting our perspective on life and directing our behaviors, we may become susceptible to depression, anxiety, anger, apathy, or desperation (to name only a few possibilities).

At a conscious level we ascribe meaning to events, people, places, gestures, objects, and environmental conditions (e.g., stress) given our emotional state, prior experience, knowledge base, and what we believe to be true, which is why no two people have the same accounting of a single event; each of us *perceives* an event through our own unique conscious *and* unconscious processing of information. What we tell ourselves, our *internal dialogue*, reflects this processing and greatly influences our lives, especially how we form relationships, assess situations, make decisions, solve problems, and cope with the stress that often accompanies change. We respond to change according to how we process, and ultimately internalize in words, the meaning of change in our lives.

Internal Dialogue

Mothers who perceive the changes inherent to motherhood as a natural and evolving process tell themselves exactly that. They tell themselves that life circumstances have changed, but they will retain the important aspects of themselves or their lives (however altered they may be). Likewise they tell themselves that it is all right to postpone certain goals, activities, etc., until a time that is less demanding on them. They make choices and act in a manner that supports what they believe to be true, all without a trace of resentment. Because they perceive change as a process, they tend to transition into their new role as mother without the effect of change compromising their sense of self. In fact, some women actually welcome the changes associated with motherhood and experience a heightened sense of self after a baby, regardless of the kinds of changes that occur.

Harriet's internal dialogue

This is where I belong now. This is a fleeting moment in my life and I want to experience it well before it's over. Hallie and Ryan need me, but they will not always need me so much. This time goes by so fast. I see them changing every day. I'll get through the tough spots. This is hard work, but so too would be many other things I would choose to do in my life, other things that are a lot less rewarding.

Ann's internal dialogue

I feel like I'm changing along with my kids. Some of the changes are good and some not so good. I like to see the good changes, hate the bad ones, but I recognize them as things to work on. I feel challenged in my role as mother. When I feel like quitting, I think of the role model I've become and then I want to get my head together and make this time of life a good one. Part of life is feeling stretched to do things that don't always feel good. Parenting is hard work, but I think of my relationship with my children as symbiotic; we push and pull each other to become more every day.

Conversely, a large number of mothers perceive the changes associated with motherhood as losses, which is evident in their internal dialogue. The internal dialogues that these mothers describe sound much like mantras in that the same words are used often and with focused conviction. The dialogues reflect many of the emotions that accompany a sense of longing. Unlike mantras, though, no other person can hear or dispute the typically negative words that are chosen for private thought, and as such no one can argue, reassure, or prompt an appropriate reality check. Below are a few examples of internal dialogues from mothers who wouldn't dream of voicing such words aloud unless under strict codes of confidentiality—internal dialogues that indisputably relate to the perception of change as loss. I asked, "What are some of the things you tell yourself on a regular basis?"

Theresa's internal dialogue

I just want my life back. This is too hard. They [the children] are driving me crazy. I can't do this anymore. I just can't do this anymore. I didn't know how different my life would be. I didn't want it to be so different.

Michelle's internal dialogue

I want to leave. But if I leave, I'd have to figure out a way, somehow a way where they wouldn't know where to find me. Like with my mail. How would I get my mail without them tracing me? I've just had enough. I'm not happy. Every day I'm not happy. I love my kids, but I feel like I'm dying. I'm living in a world that's not me. I'm living in a world that takes and takes from me and I have nothing left. I barely get through the day only to face another day.

Eileen's internal dialogue

How do other mothers do it? What am I doing wrong? Is it just me? Why am I having such trouble doing this? What happened to me? I shouldn't have been a mother. I stink at this.

Lisa's internal dialogue

I feel helpless, like I can't get what I want. Teddy [her husband] has a life. I want my life. He comes home and seems happy enough. I know he has his share of stress every day, but he's always being praised for what he is doing for us, affording us a nice home, etc. He gets stroked, every day. He gets a great sense of fulfillment every day. He gets a sense of accomplishment every day. I get nothing. Every day I work at home and I feel like what I do amounts to nothing. Every day I do the same things—cleaning, cooking, changing diapers. It's like running on a treadmill. There's never a sense of accomplishment because the same things have to be done every day. Yeah, I know, it's good the kids have a parent at home, and I know I'm probably doing the right thing by them, but this stinks.

Kendra

I have no life of my own. I think that's what I always say because it's true. I don't have a life of my own. I just don't. I don't think most mothers do.

Sharon

I don't know how to change things. I'm stuck in some bad ways. This is not how I want life. I can't think of how to change things. Every day Michael [her husband] and I do the same things. I want things to change, change some things so that life gets a little easier for me. I want him to take on more of the responsibility. I can't do it all. It's too much. But I can't think of how to change or what to change to get what I want. I can't even think anymore. I'm stuck. I'm trapped. I can't get out of this. I can't change this.

Verbal and Nonverbal Language

Apart from giving a voice to internal dialogues, many mothers openly and willingly shared their feelings aloud. In just about every interview discussing these feelings, mothers began with similar assertions of love, as if to weaken the potency of words to come. Once love, gratitude, awe, and joy were out of the way, I heard the raw and honest feelings that mothers can have when unencumbered by the expectations typically associated with the role of mother.

Peggy summed it up in the fewest words:

There's no room for me in my own life.

In her response, Peggy suggested that she was missing from her life (hence, the play on words in the acronym MIA). On further exploration, I found out that Peggy spent an inordinate amount of time on housework, homework, carpooling, and childcare. Little was left of the life and person Peggy once knew before children and so we hear the resentment, anger, depression, or disappointment that claims her comment. Although having children was indescribable to her in terms of joy, the radical changes that occurred along with her passage into motherhood generated various kinds of feelings, even feelings she was hesitant to own.

Claire

I feel like a marathon runner who ran out of steam miles before the finish line. I want to cross the finish line every day, but sometimes I fall short of energy to do what I've got to do. I do it, but I drag myself and literally collapse after all three [children] are in bed. They take every ounce of me, every ounce. [She sits rubbing her forehead with one hand while obsessively rocking her left leg.] *I could be lying in bed bleeding to death and I know one of them would ask me to do something as if nothing were wrong. It's like they only think of me as someone who does for them, and they get mad if I don't do what they need, regardless of the blood I was spilling. Children are so self-absorbed.* [She smirks.]

Lynn

Motherhood is not at all what I thought it would be. I look at old photos and see all the smiles and love. I do love them very much. Really can't imagine how my life would be without them. But sometimes I do imagine it. [She smiles a guilty grin.] *I wish I could live a double life. Have an apartment of my own somewhere and be able to go to it when I want to. I want to see them [the children] and even take care of them, but I've got to tell you. It's taking its toll on me. I can't even finish a thought, it seems. I hate not having time for myself. I hate not taking care of myself in ways I know I need to. I hate feeling like a housemaid. I hate that my husband resents me for not giving him attention, and I hate the tension that exists in this house when I feel so desperate. And I do feel desperate at times, desperate to look in the mirror and recognize who I see, and like that person I see.*

Lynn expresses what I refer to as conflicting feelings. Conflicting feelings confuse mothers most. They are periodic feelings of resentment, anger, hate, anxiety, regret, despair, and other feelings that seemingly contradict the love they have for their children. As heartbreaking as these feelings may be to experience, they are quite common among mothers. Typically mothers come face-to-face with conflicting feelings when coping with extremes, such as extreme fatigue or frustration. I know when I was pushed beyond my capacity to cope or when my needs were consistently not being met, words would slip from my mouth that I knew were harsh but true in the moment. Anyone listening might have said that I was an angry, resentful mother who didn't like her children. That's why I have only spewed those words under my breath or in the privacy of my bedroom while trying to compose myself. Likewise, my conflicting feelings emerged when I felt burned out, when I couldn't interrupt another tantrum or settle an argument over a twenty-five-cent piece of junk the girls bought from the arcade at the supermarket, a very ugly incident indeed; I lost control in the parking lot, yelling about the cheap necklace that would certainly break by evening and my desire to be "free" again, wandering solo through parks and malls and anywhere I wanted to go, when I wanted to go, for as long as I wanted to go, untouched by the details and nonsense of children. Of course, as conflicting feelings go, within the hour I was regretting that I ever spoke those words aloud.

At the root of conflicting feelings exists the mental anguish that accompanies a mother's diminishing sense of self; this mental anguish is grief. Having conflicting feelings toward one's child does not suggest a lack of love nor does it reflect the decision to have children or the desire to live another lifestyle. Rather, it's the grief over the loss of self that causes mothers to know the conflicting feelings they battle; moments of extreme fatigue or frustration merely expose the grief because in those moments mothers usually feel as out of touch with themselves as they can possibly feel. There is nothing left to give. The well was never filled, so to speak, and now it's dry, especially for Mom. Anyone listening closely would hear the questions these mothers ask under their breath, questions that begin with "why," "when," and "what," as in "Why did I have children?" or "When do I get my life back?" or "What happened to me?" These kinds of questions illuminate conflict, the natural conflict that exists between the sacrifices that are required of a mother and a mother's desire to preserve her sense of self. When circumstances tilt the extraordinary balance needed to assuage this conflict, mothers slowly lose their sense of self and generally confront the conflicting feelings associated with Maternal Intrapersonal Anxiety (MIA).

Symptoms

Internal dialogues and conflicting feelings generate what I refer to as the emotional responses or symptoms related to motherhood. Herein lies the place for depression, anxiety, sadness, frustration, anger/resentment, guilt/shame, lack of self-concern, decreased self-esteem, irritability, mood swings, self-doubt, abrupt or prolonged bouts of crying, self-consciousness, a feeling of helplessness or the feeling of losing one's mind, despair, denial, and, of course, loss of identity. These emotional symptoms evidenced in nearly every interview I conducted. To be sure, I always asked at least one question to confirm what I had heard, such as "Do you feel helpless?" "Do you experience sudden changes in mood?" However, a mother's physical, cognitive, and behavioral symptoms factor in as well when assessing how she perceives the changes that occurred in her life in the first few years of motherhood. And so, I explored these kinds of symptoms.

Janet (physical)

I'm certainly tired all the time. Physically I'm not what I used to be. I guess because I'm run-down. I get sick a lot. I get a lot of headaches and body aches. I'm just tired.

Erin (psychological)

I feel very hormonal. That means emotional. I go anywhere from crying to screaming in the course of a day. I always feel on the edge, always ready to snap.

Heather (physical)

I've got all kinds of health problems. Most recently I was diagnosed with MS. MS? How'd I get MS? My doctor says it's stress-related. [She sighs, pauses, then continues.] *Honestly, I think the stress of staying home every day with my children has a lot to do with this.*

Lisa M. (social/behavioral)

I'm not as outgoing as I used to be. I used to see my friends all the time, hang out, laugh. Now I just don't feel like it. I feel like staying home. I don't know why. I just don't want to see my friends like I used to.

Ann (cognitive)

I know my memory sucks. Maybe I have too many little things on my mind with all the kid stuff, but I forget a lot of things. I try to be organized. I keep lists, but it makes no difference. I'm more scattered than anything, more scattered than any other time in my life. I'm just all over the place. Can't seem to keep a straight thought.

Helena (psychological/behavioral)

Well, I kind of feel ashamed to say this, but I've been on an antidepressant. I was feeling so depressed for no reason I could put my finger on. I tried to get through it. I thought it would pass. It got to the point where I was too tired to fake it anymore. I knew I needed help and I figured this would be temporary. I just want help to get through this. I'm having a hard time of it.

Dianne (psychological)

For me, it was all about my identity. The shift from an active and successful lawyer to mother proved harder than I imagined. I was esteemed in my practice and loved what I did. I was a much-sought-after attorney, and I liked how that made me feel. I only realized that after I left my practice. I have not adjusted well to motherhood. I don't feel attached to my role as mother. It's almost like it doesn't fit me well. I believe I'll do a good job, but I look around most days and wonder if I'm in the Twilight Zone. This doesn't feel real in a way. I'm not comfortable yet, I suppose. [A long pause.] I'm not sure who I am at the moment. Certainly not a lawyer.

Janine (cognitive)

I have all kinds of symptoms. I wouldn't know where to begin. But you struck a chord when you mentioned thinking patterns. I've become so negative. My husband tends to call attention to the times I say that I can't do something. And it's never really anything I literally cannot do. I guess I'm just saying that out of frustration or anger or any of the other feelings that I have during the day. I know I say, "I can't do this anymore" a lot. Again, its out of frustration, I'm sure.

The symptoms in the stories above parallel the most common symptoms experienced in people who are grieving a significant loss in their lives (in Chapter 3 I list the symptoms most associated with grief-stricken individuals for the sake of comparison). While I understand and thoroughly appreciate how mothers can experience enough stress day-to-day from childcare and household responsibilities to prompt the negative internal dialogues, conflicting feelings, and symptoms they describe, I also believe a greater source of stress exists when this kind of feedback occurs simultaneously, with great intensity, or more than occasionally.

I argue that the *greater* source of stress for so many mothers dwells in the impact of losing their sense of self, whether mothers are consciously aware of it or not. A mother's sense of self incorporates at least four different concepts of self. Her actual self reflects who she is in the present state and what she portrays to others, such as her age or profession. This differs from her ideal self, which is the image of who she wants to be. Her private self is how she perceives herself as being or would like to be; that is, how she acts as a person (e.g., funny, sincere, competitive). And, of course, her social self is how she would like to be seen by others (e.g., attractive, responsible, capable, strong). These four concepts of self give form to her overall sense of self, which develops over the years out of the culmination of events, people, values, perceptions, images, roles, personality traits, and inherent characteristics that establish her as a distinct and unique individual relative to others. A threat to the integrity of her sense of self is likely to impact many facets of her life and cause her to feel many things. However, for grief to exist, a woman must perceive any lost sense of self as the loss of an emotional attachment. The question is, can we be emotionally attached to our sense of self?

R. Scott Sullender, a pastoral counselor, describes how we inevitably form emotional attachments to many things as a network toward becoming fully functional and emotionally sound adults. As an analogy he uses the image of a spider at the center of its web, the strands of the web representing our emotional attachments in all directions and in varying intensities. Sullender claims that should an emotional attachment break, we will experience symptoms of grief relative to the *value* we gave the emotional attachment. "Value" is as key here as the concept of attachment. In terms of value, I know I value my role as daughter, wife, mother, sister, teacher, writer, and friend as I value each loved one related to those roles. I also value my self-esteem, my sense of humor, my health, my independence, my artistic talent, and my wanderlust as I value other aspects of my life, such as a nice home and the money that provides my family with a comfortable living. Perhaps differently and to different degrees, but I do value *all* the people and things that contribute to my life in a meaningful way. Similarly, I know my experience of grief will vary according to the value and meaning I give to a particular aspect of my life. However, whether I lose a significant person through death, divorce, or broken friendship, or a valued external object, such as my home or a special memento, I will grieve. I will also grieve should I lose a physical aspect of myself, such as a body part to illness/injury or a non-physical aspect, such as my loss of status, self-worth, an anticipated outcome, a goal/dream, or an opportunity. In other words, when the concept of "me" is jeopardized in any way or for any duration, I will respond and generate symptoms most often observed and reported during times of grief. I will grieve because I am emotionally attached to what was jeopardized, that is, "me."

Having said this, the basic framework in which I am working considers all emotional attachments to people, places, objects, concepts, images, beliefs, personal attributes and characteristics, etc., as similar in the context of what most people value. We become emotionally attached to what we value. If we develop emotional attachments to all that contribute to our sense of self (all that we value), then it stands to reason that we would be emotionally attached to that sense of self. This being the case, a mother may grieve aspects of her self and her life that she lost since becoming a mother much the way she would grieve more obvious losses or the loss of any other valued component of her life.

TWO:
WHAT'S THERE TO LOSE?

"For many persons, the loss occasioned by death is the only loss worthy of significant attention; but the losses to which we do not pay intentional heed may have a more profound impact on us in the long run."

—*Kenneth R. Mitchell and Herbert Anderson,* **All Our Losses,
All Our Griefs**

Mothers don't usually consider a lost sense of self as a reason for their negative self-talk, conflicting feelings, or symptoms probably because the whole concept of self, one's sense of self, is so abstract and elusive. And then to talk about losing that sense of self, well, that may be pushing things. Another reason might involve the fact that childbirth is usually thought of as an occasion to be joyfully anticipated, celebrated, and embraced in its entirety. To introduce a negative consequence of having a baby might raise a few eyebrows, and no one wants to do that. But the truth is, having a baby changes everything, and mothers learn this quite quickly. It's even something Johnson & Johnson clearly advertises. Of course J & J shows the sweeter, gentler moments that babies fill in the lives of their parents, but the reality of a baby is far more complicated than a twenty-second commercial intended to entice its viewing public. Having a baby and caring for the child that he or she becomes is hard work and involves many tough moments. Unfortunately, mothers rarely talk about these tough times and in that tacit way become vulnerable to society's skewed perception that they have the "luxury" of staying home with their children as though it should be a welcomed situation that bears no burdens.

I've taken the time to speak with men, women, and mothers who work full-time outside the home, and it never ceases to amaze me when I hear comments that expose envy and mistaken ideals. Once I overheard a conversation my husband had with several acquaintances he knew from a theater group. He was asked if his wife worked. He answered, "Yes, she works full-time at home with our three children." Although I smiled upon hearing this because I knew I had duly influenced him over the years, I was nevertheless disheartened when I heard their responses. "Yes, but does she work?" Again my husband said, "Yes, at home." This went on for several minutes with my husband having to "defend" me. It was clear that their inquisition went beyond curiosity and toward a kind of resentment that is hard to put into words. I wanted to scream from the other room, "Yes, I !@#&*% work. In fact, I never *not* work. I move from chore to chore all day without a word of praise or gratitude. I work two twelve-hour shifts *every* day and eat my meals while standing and serving others. I receive no paycheck for my efforts or any medical benefits. I can never quit (or get fired!), call in sick, get a paid vacation, or receive a pension for the many years I devoted to my work. My work is tedious, demanding, and all-consuming, and yet others think nothing of judging me or criticizing me for doing what they could not (or do not) do." Needless to say, I felt angry and somewhat self-conscious, as though I should question what I was doing at home with my children. Given such subtle (and unfortunate) messages from society, mothers may ignore, deny, or stifle any feelings that reflect a personal crisis related to motherhood.

Mothers also obscure their feelings and symptoms by keeping busy with all the chores, distractions, and commitments that call them. While they answer the call of motherhood, they tend to miss the greater process unfolding within them; that is, the process of letting go of the women they were and a time that existed before they had children. This is a process that's imperative to attend; the process of letting go is a valid component of change. In some changes that occur in the first few years of motherhood, mothers can incorporate the old with the new. But in most instances, change means moving from one state of being to another or from one set of circumstances to another. Regardless of the kind of change, mothers must often let go of what was, even if temporarily. Letting go, by its very nature, suggests loss. So it should come as no surprise that mothers might feel a sense of loss for what they no longer have. "Having a baby changes everything." For indeed it does, as mothers know best. But what mothers may not know (understand or appreciate) is exactly how the changes in everything often involve loss and how loss affects their lives. Toward this end, I cite six major kinds of loss that generally occur *over the course of a lifetime*. But as I have discovered, these six kinds of loss also seem to occur *simultaneously* for many women during the first few years of motherhood, making grief a legitimate cause for consideration. I offer examples of each kind of loss from mothers I interviewed or from mothers who agreed to meet at my house as part of a focus group. These losses include material loss, relationship loss, intrapsychic loss, functional loss, role loss, and systemic loss.

Material Loss

A material loss occurs when an important physical object or familiar surrounding is lost. In this category, income is included. Many women lose an income when they leave the workforce to stay at home full-time. Loss of income accompanies a loss of financial independence, which often affects self-esteem and rattles one's sense of self. As for other examples, Janine cited the exchange of her sports car for the minivan that more comfortably hosts her new little family; Michelle talked about the quaint home that became too small for her growing children, the need for a bigger home concealing the loss of the newlywed dwelling that held fond memories. Debra elaborated on the loss of her wardrobe, a wardrobe that had become either too small for her waistline or too fancy for the day-to-day activities of a stay-at-home mom. Cathie literally cried when sharing the story of the day she had to get rid of her dog, Ramon, who was perceived by her husband as an imposing threat to their infant son. She agreed with her husband that her son's safety was most important, but she never quite reconciled with the loss of a dog she had adopted many years ago for her own protection (and company). These are losses that may seem relatively minor in nature, but new mothers may perceive them as major losses depending on the value they hold and whether or not they are accompanied by other kinds of loss.

Relationship Loss

Relationship loss seems intrinsic to motherhood unless I misinterpreted the loud groans and sighs that filled the air as I described this loss to the group of mothers invited to my house. I could fill a separate book with all the stories these mothers have shared about their experiences with relationship loss. According to Mitchell and Anderson, authors of *All Our Losses, All Our Griefs*, relationship loss is "the ending of opportunities to relate oneself to, talk with, share experiences with, make love to, touch, settle issues with, fight with, and otherwise be in the emotional and/or physical presence of a particular other human being."

Marianne offers her perspective on a relationship loss:

My mother and I had always been close even though she always had such a strong will. I figured she'd have a lot to say once my baby came along, and she did. So often I heard about how she did things when she was a new mom, as if to tell me how to do things with my baby. I would listen, taking her advice sometimes, and sometimes not. Well, one day she and I totally disagreed with how to discipline my son, who was having lots of tantrums. She said things that really bothered me and I didn't know how to stand my ground; I just got really angry with her and didn't talk to her for months. It was awkward but neither of us made a move to fix things. I did feel a loss. I felt sad and angry that she couldn't appreciate that I was a mother as well and I could discipline my own child the way I thought was appropriate. I figured we'd eventually talk. I wanted to have a good relationship with my mother, especially now, but I could feel the strain between us soon after the baby came along. I just didn't know how to explain my feelings, I suppose. As time went on we did start talking again, but I always had one reason after another for not addressing the problems between us, which, by the way, are still here.

In this example, Marianne highlights a loss of relationship with her mother. I asked Marianne what "reasons" kept her from reconciling with her mother, and she said, "Mostly that I'm too tired or too busy. I need lots of energy and nerve to confront people, and I don't have much of either these days." Although Marianne wants a good relationship with her mother, she claims that fatigue, a busy schedule, and nerve prevent her from pursuing that better relationship. Beyond these reasons, one could easily argue that Marianne has poor communication skills or low self-esteem, both of which prevent her from expressing her needs and expectations. The point is that Marianne *believes* it's her fatigue, "nerve," and busy schedule that keep her from having the kind of relationship she wants with her mother. Marianne's perception is that her life circumstances changed. She became a mother, she became busy and tired, and she lost a relationship with her mother for these reasons. In change came loss.

Ann shares her experience:

No doubt my friendships suffered. You're just too busy to maintain some friendships. My new friends are other moms, but I do miss my old friends. None of them have children yet. Maybe we'll connect again if ever they do have kids. But right now, we have very different lives. They go out, they're free to do what they want, when they want to. I can't keep up with that. I can't go out with them anymore. They're still going to bars to drink and dance, and probably meet men. It's not my world anymore.

Liz shares her feelings:

My husband and I are not the same. And so our relationship is not the same, which I suppose is a natural process after a baby is born. We're close, definitely committed, but less happy, I think, overall with our relationship. Of course, there is less intimacy, which doesn't help, and then he comes home tired and I'm tired and so we talk a little before we turn in for the night. Life was never like that before the kids came along.

Spousal relationships suffered most with friendships and familial relationships fighting for second place. In my own experience of friendship loss, I remember how it felt when Jim and I moved away from our little apartment building full of friends in downtown Princeton, NJ. We were no longer able to step out our door and be within a community of people that we had come to enjoy and depend on. The physical distance of our move proved taxing on the close bonds of friendship that we had established while pursuing our education. Of course all of us could have put forth the effort to maintain the relationships we developed, but as most people know, it's easy to lose touch with even the closest friends when travel is necessary and babies are demanding. At the time, I didn't acknowledge my loss of friendships. Neither time, nor energy, nor the capacity to think of much else other than my new daughter allowed loss to enter as a reality infringing upon my mental health.

Being no exception to the rule, I also experienced a relationship loss with my husband. He and I were fortunate enough to have remained committed and emotionally close, but the combined effects of fatigue, distractions, teething, work, and little sex drive did come between us as we struggled to adjust and redefine our relationship. During our first few years as parents, I know that I wasn't nearly as physically affectionate toward my husband as I had been over the years that preceded parenthood. There was no apparent reason for this other than the fact that I was preoccupied with my new baby and exhausted from all the attention she required. By the time I was ready for bed at night, I desired nothing but the warmth and comfort of the flannel sheets that had no expectation of me; I couldn't wait to turn off the world and rest. My relationship with my husband turned and twisted for many reasons, and was virtually lost in the chaos of early parenthood. The days of hanging out having intimate dinners and snuggling for hours was traded in for different ways of sharing time. Fortunately, over the years, we were able to re-create our relationship. We renewed our commitment to each other, we focused on our growing family, and we incorporated the kind of love that endures the drastic change of self that parenthood fosters.

Intrapsychic Loss

> *"We will mourn the loss of others. But we are also going to mourn the loss of our selves—of earlier definitions that our images of self depend upon. For the changes in our body redefine us. The events of our personal history rede-fine us. The ways that others perceive us redefine us. And at several points in our life we will have to relinquish a former self-image and move on."*
>
> —*Judith Viorst,* **Necessary Losses**

Intrapsychic loss represented the most profound loss for the mothers in my focus group. It's the loss on which this book is based. Intrapsychic loss is "the experience of losing an emotionally important image of oneself, losing the possi-bilities of what might have been, abandonment of plans for a particular future, the dying of a dream…. It is itself an entirely inward experience," write Marshall and Anderson. This kind of loss typically parallels times of change. For instance, mothers may experience an intrapsychic loss as the result of the "empty nest syn-drome"; however, a similar experience exists for many mothers at the other end of the spectrum when a baby enters the "nest." Without question the onset of change and the awesome experience of having a baby coaxed me steadily away from what I wanted for myself in terms of personal goals and accomplishments. Similar to my knee flinching when tested for reflexes, I responded to my baby in kind. To every noise, every need, I reacted without thought. I did, and did some more, all the tasks without questioning where I stood in the picture and what I wanted from my own life. I wonder now how I could have let that happen, but I think the answer lies somewhere in the power of love and my desire to do all the right things for the baby that was entrusted to me.

Linda's experience of intrapsychic loss

I had always thought of myself as a dancer. I've danced since I was a kid. I moved from Pittsburgh about eight years ago to train in New York. Dan and I weren't even married when I got pregnant. We didn't plan it, but we decided to keep the baby. It's amazing how drastically things changed. It was a difficult birth and the baby was very colicky. No one plans or expects that. Colic is terrible, terribly draining for parents. Anyway, a whole year passed and I never danced. I figured I was still adjusting, but here we are three and a half years later and guess what? No, I'm not dancing. It hurts not to dance, literally. I know I will never be the dancer I dreamed of becoming, and I know I'm getting too old to perform, or compete to perform, in the [NYC] shows I had once hoped to be in. Too much time has passed and I'm not the athlete I once was. But hopefully I'll at least take some dance classes in the future and feel that joy in my life again.

Mary Ann's experience

For me, it was just being a professional woman. I loved dressing up every day. Nice clothes, nice hairstyles, a little perfume, a little makeup. It was the whole image. Leave the house with a briefcase, get into a nice car, stop for coffee at Starbucks before getting to the office. You see, it's the whole experience I miss. I might eventually go back to work, but I've heard many women say the same thing, and they never do for one reason or another. Or they go back but the experience is not the same. Right now I have my hands full with the kids. I'm glad I'm home with them, but I certainly do miss the life I had. I miss the look, the feel, the friends, the whole thing.

The mothers in my focus group could now identify an experience that they could not formerly articulate. All of them could relate to letting go of an important image of themselves or letting go of a personal ambition either altogether or for a considerable amount of time. While fathers may alter their priorities and goals once a baby comes along, they usually continue working toward fulfilling the career goals they set prior to parenthood. On the other hand, mothers often surrender their career goals completely or at least until their children are older and more independent. This time lapse often sabotages the trajectory of a career set in motion before motherhood and defuses the skills necessary to jump back in where one left off. Interestingly, some women from my mothers group claimed that their self-perceptions denied them the career opportunities that still remained; in other words, opportunity existed but confidence didn't.

My sister, Betty, represents for me the ideal example of altered ambition and intrapsychic loss. She is a mother of two, and decided to be a stay-at-home mom without deliberation. She remains one of the most devoted mothers I know, dedicating her time to the execution of details that she hopes will secure her children's success, socially, educationally, and otherwise. She's invested in everything they do and is involved in as many activities as possible that relate to them. Graduating first in her class from Manhattan's prestigious fine arts college Fashion Institute of Technology, Betty continues to draw on her skills when making Christmas cards by hand and in all the crafts Girl Scouts make when under her leadership. Her creativity surges around holidays, birthdays, and any event that demands color, vitality, and imagination.

I watch Betty sometimes when she doesn't know I'm there, and I can still see the young woman who worked diligently in school to perfect the project that earned her (above all others in her class) the opportunity to attend the Aspen Design Conference in Colorado. She was amazing. And still is, but for reasons I would not have suspected while daydreaming with her long before her children came along. I have to admit that I have mourned for her, for I have never once heard an ounce of regret in her voice regarding the choices she made years ago to leave the world of art for the children who called her Mommy. On rare occasion she and I have talked about her return to a field that exercised her talents, but she insisted that she had become too different and too "out of touch" with how her field has evolved electronically. I, on the other hand, have always insisted back to her that her children have only glimpsed the incredibly talented designer that lives inside her, the designer content to create for them and not for the recognition, accolades, and acclaim that would have certainly been hers had she made different choices. I don't think she made a bad choice in staying home with her children; in fact I respect her decision wholeheartedly, but somehow it's still hard for me never to have seen this especially talented woman fully develop as the designer she once aspired to be.

Functional Loss

Functional loss is the fourth type of loss and the one that raised the most eyebrows. "Functional loss?" "Did I experience that too without knowing it?" Yes for some mothers and no for most mothers when questioned during my interviews. This loss results from muscular and neurological dysfunction of one's body. This type of loss does not typically occur over the course of a woman's transition into motherhood. However, some mothers suffered a functional loss because of a difficult labor and delivery that required an episiotomy. Poorly performed episiotomies caused the lasting physical damage and impaired sexual function that these mothers have known. Similarly, a small percentage of mothers described a significant decrease in nipple sensation, which was the result of the months and years they devoted to nursing their children. Sleep deprivation and sleep disturbances also fall into this category. Most new mothers go without a solid night's sleep for many months. They usually wake to feed a hungry baby or soothe a frightened one. Sleep deprivation has been linked to irritability, blurred vision, slurred speech, memory lapses, decreased sex drive, nausea, and an overall feeling of confusion. Most dramatic, though, were the number of mothers who live with a condition called "stress incontinence," a loss of bladder control that was described as embarrassing, inconvenient, and upsetting. Stress incontinence is the release of urine upon exertion when exercising, sneezing, or doing anything that creates an unexpected jolt to the body. These mothers openly shared their distress in having to wear protection against this bothersome consequence of childbirth and the functional loss it created.

Colleen's experience

Aw, it's terrible. I had no idea something like this could happen. Nobody ever told me something like this could happen. And it's not that rare. We don't like to talk about it but it happens. I could barely walk across the room without [she pauses and makes a funny face] *leaking. How embarrassing.*

Role Loss

The remaining types of loss are independent of each other yet overlap to a large degree. They are role loss and systemic loss. A role loss is "the loss of a specific social role or of one's accustomed place in a social network," according to Marshall and Anderson. Role loss is experienced when one's place (status) in a social context is altered by change. Retirement is often used in books as the ideal example. In retirement, one leaves the workplace and all the familiarities therein. It's a transition that involves a shifting image, a shift that is often associated with the loss of friendships/camaraderie, money, status, power/influence, intellectual stimulation, and frequently, self-esteem. Another example of role loss cited in literature is when a single person marries. However, the women I interviewed who had children after getting married emphasized the greater role loss they experienced after they became mothers. They stressed that the transition into their role as mothers was far more intense and life-altering than the transition into their role as wives; they claimed that their social lives (friendships/camaraderie), psychological well-being (sense of power/influence, self-esteem), financial status (money), personal development (intellectual stimulation, ambitions/goals), and physical stature were *instantly* altered and more dramatically changed after becoming mothers than at the moment in which they became wives. (Note the similarities between motherhood and the experience of retirement!) That is, shifting from the role of single woman to married woman was far less traumatic than shifting from the role of married woman without child to married woman with child (mother); in short, becoming a mother impacts role change to a greater degree, thus creating the greater likelihood of role loss. I mention this strictly to demonstrate how motherhood is generally overlooked when the concept of loss appears in literature. Early motherhood is a time when women experience several kinds of loss, most of which are never considered. This fact reflects our great oversight as a society in recognizing the dynamics that take place when women become mothers. If it's not an oversight, then perhaps it's sheer ignorance or indifference.

Debra C. shares her experience:

Over the years I was always the one people called if there was a party to be had. I love to host and I think I do it well. If I wasn't hosting the parties, I was going to them. I have a lot of friends and family. But ever since I had Katie, my friends rarely call me to either socialize or entertain. And my family, well, I see them and I talk to them, but when it comes to holidays and gatherings, they'd rather have it elsewhere now.

When I offered Debra my opinion that her friends and family might be genuinely trying to consider her new situation, Debra replied, "It's still hurtful." I imagine a group of close friends neglecting to call when having a few drinks after work can be hurtful. Likewise, when family members decide among themselves to trade the tradition of Christmas dinner at one home in favor of another home where there is less commotion caused by young children. Of course family and friends usually have only the best intentions in mind, but best intentions aside, these examples demonstrate how a shift in one's role within a family or group of friends can nevertheless be experienced as a loss that hurts.

Nancy shares her thoughts:

I was a supervisor before I had Connor. I enjoyed my job. The hours were good, pay was decent, and I liked the people I worked with. I liked that the staff looked to me to either teach them new skills or create the structure we needed to do well against the competition. When I left, I felt ready. I wanted a baby and knew that I wanted to be home full-time with the baby. But, boy, were things different. In the beginning it was all right. That honeymoon stage was great. I was in my own world. But I started to notice things that made me feel bad. Like every time my husband and I socialized, the conversation seemed to always be directed to him, as though I had nothing important to say anymore. I would mention the baby and everyone would just nod and say a few things before moving on again in conversation. And the tone of their voices would make you think they were just humoring me, even though I don't think they were. Yuck. I think I kind of felt stupid. Like why was I even trying to make conversation? [Pause] Here I was an ex-supervisor of a major corporation who decided to stay home with her new baby. It didn't make me boring or less important. But that's how I felt, I guess.

Nancy's perception of the status change (i.e., loss of status) in her life after a baby is common among a large number of women who leave the workforce to raise their children. In interview after interview I heard similar comments of a transition that arrived as a choice but resulted in an unanticipated drop in self-esteem. Choosing what they thought was good for their children turned out to be a decision that caused many mothers to feel "less than" others, especially compared to other women who remained in the workforce, with or without a child at home. Unfortunately, this happens because society esteems many things that mothers typically are not. Influenced by media, society tends to esteem wealth, independence, sex appeal, fame, excitement, success, and power. Mothers simply don't fit the profile. As much as society wishes to encourage and embrace mothers in their decision to stay at home with their young children, they undermine those wishes with subtle messages to the contrary; messages that mothers often hear and integrate in adverse ways.

Systemic Loss

Systemic loss relates to role loss because the roles we play are *always* within the context of a larger system. As a supervisor, a woman relates to her staff within the context of a business; as a friend, a woman relates within the context of her friendships, and as a daughter, sister, aunt, and wife a woman relates within the context of her family. In the latter example the family is the larger system. Within the family system, a woman interacts with other family members in a style of communication (verbal and nonverbal) that is unique to that particular family; the family comes to *depend on* the status quo of communication to which it has become accustomed. When role loss affects a woman and incites a change in her behavior or mood (i.e., symptoms of grief), she inadvertently disturbs the status quo given the interactive nature of the family system. As a result, the entire family experiences the effects of loss along with the woman. A loss for one member of the family affects every other member of the family system; that is, the whole family shows signs of grief. In this way role loss and systemic loss are separate constructs, yet enmeshed in effect. Systemic loss merely scopes the larger effect of change, loss, and grief.

Sheila M.

I know I'm not happy. I feel disoriented. One minute I'm in a skirt and heels and the next minute I have a toddler throwing a book at me because he's mad that I have to take him food shopping with me. I mean, what's going on? In so many ways he acts like I feel. But I try to keep it together. I try to be patient. I suppose that he's going through his growing pains and I'm going through mine, and we clash a lot. He throws books and I cry. Worst thing is, I don't have the energy to stop him. And we just keep feeding off each other's bad energy. Him with the tantrums and me with the tears.

I could cite several more stories from mothers I interviewed that reflect sys-temic loss, but for riveting examples that clearly demonstrate the effects of loss and grief within the family, watch the television show *Nanny 911* or *The Super Nanny*. Each show **capitalizes** on the systemic nature of loss. My construct of MIA would suggest that the demands of childcare and running a home (along with the perceived losses associated with motherhood) have pounded the sense of self right out of the mothers depicted in each episode. They stand among their families as helpless and desperate women, aching from their grief. Their children are out of control, acting on the emotions circulating within the household. Each family member is stressed out, putting his or her own spin on the grief that is painfully apparent in the mother. A loss for one member of the family (e.g., a mother's lost sense of self) affects every other member of the family system; that is systemic loss.

Inherent Elements of Loss

Beyond the six major kinds of loss mentioned above, Mitchell and Anderson describe inherent elements of loss itself, which must be considered since they fur-ther define the experience of loss. Four categories exist: avoidable and unavoid-able; temporary and permanent; anticipated and unanticipated; actual and imagined. Many examples of avoidable/unavoidable loss exist in the lifestyle one chooses. If one *chooses* a particular lifestyle, it's *assumed* that he or she accepts the consequences (good and bad) that result from that decision. Unfortunately, power of choice seems to determine the degree of sympathy and support one receives when loss is present. Perhaps this would explain why our society tends to slight the losses related to motherhood while embracing the losses related to retirement, losses such as friendships, money, status, and self-worth. Whereas women usually choose to have babies, retirees don't choose to age, thus there is more sympathy for those retiring than there is for women who become mothers. The truth is, we cannot predict every loss, nor can value always be known until that moment when something we love is lost. As the popular expression goes, "I didn't know what I had until I lost it." Such is usually the case, which should render the issue of choice irrelevant when considering the effects of loss and the support one expects when trying to cope with those losses.

Examples of temporary loss for women entering motherhood might include weight gain, income, and spousal intimacy, whereas stress incontinence (and other functional losses), breast size/shape, and certain material losses are more likely examples of permanent loss. Interestingly, a temporary loss may be more difficult to reconcile with because the word "temporary" means that something will be recovered or regained sometime in the future. But a vague concept of time with an implied promise of relief offers very little to a weary mom who is battling constant disappointment or feelings of failure. On the contrary, a permanent loss offers no promise and yet it's that exact reality that helps a person eventually move beyond grief. Given this irony, mothers may actually grieve their temporary losses more than they grieve their permanent losses.

Anticipated and unanticipated losses are yet another category that reflects an intrinsic feature of loss. As an example, I anticipated that I would not have the same sense of freedom after I had a baby, but I didn't anticipate how having a baby would adversely affect my self-esteem, the friendships that I had already established with women who didn't have children, or the relationship I had with my husband. The Penn State Child and Family Development Project supports the potentially adverse effect of children on marriages in their finding that one out of every two marriages begin having trouble after a baby arrives and that the women experience the decline first and most dramatically. The mothers in my "findings" did not anticipate the stress of parenthood on their marriages, nor did they anticipate several of the other changes in their lives that equate to loss.

The final category of inherent elements of loss considers whether or not a loss is actual or imagined. Whereas an actual loss may be the "worst fears come true," an imagined loss feels as though the worst fears came true but in reality hasn't come true at all. The fear of loss creates the imagined loss. For example, a woman may fear that her husband is being unfaithful in the first few months of parenthood since intimacy between partners tends to decline during this time. Her feelings may escalate to the point where there is no distinction between the loss she fears (the imagined loss) and the actual loss associated with such infidelity. The imagined loss is internalized as an actual loss, even though nothing more may be going on than self-deception. Hence, a woman will grieve in much the same way as any of the other kinds of loss listed above.

The six different kinds of loss that relate to motherhood combined with the chaos, energy, and work associated with childcare jeopardize a mother's sense of self. Given the abstract nature of the self and one's sense of self, a discussion about losing "it" may prove difficult. However, it is not at all difficult to see an overlap between the six kinds of loss discussed in this chapter and the experiences mothers have shared thus far. Nor is it difficult to observe how taxing childcare can be on mothers. Oprah Winfrey and several television shows such as *Desperate Housewives* and *The Super Nanny* have greatly exposed just how taxing childcare can be. All I did was listen and note the changes that result from motherhood and how those changes affect mothers. I heard negative internal dialogues, conflicting feelings, and numerous ongoing symptoms, all of which I had heard before in my role as a grief counselor. Naturally, I concluded that mothers often experience change as loss and that their negative self-talk, feelings, and symptoms reflect grief.

THREE:
ABOUT GRIEF

"Pain becomes bearable when we are able to trust that it won't
last forever, not when we pretend that it doesn't exist."

—*Alla Bozarth-Campbell*

In the words of a true adolescent, "Grief sucks." These words came from the son
of a woman who died in the hospice where I once worked. His words were as suc-
cinct a description as I have ever heard. At the time I was relatively inexperienced
and grasping for words that would comfort him, but I knew that his pain was too
new and too deep for any words I could find that might console him in the smallest way. Instead we sat quietly for a long time surrounded by the familiar traces of
his mother. What could one say about grief? Of course no one wants it, but it is a
part of our lives and something we will experience repeatedly until the day we
die. Grief is the natural response to loss, and loss can be experienced in many
ways and in varying degrees. Most losses are obvious, such as the death of a loved
one. This loss typically receives the greatest amount of public recognition and
sympathy, and rightfully so. It is a loss that cannot escape our consciousness. But
as I've come to learn from my own experience, some losses do escape our consciousness despite their powerful calling. Whether in denial, ignorant of symptoms, or impacted by society's general intolerance for grief, many of us allow
certain losses to go unclaimed. Be that as it may, a loss occurs if an attachment is
impaired or severed. And the grief it elicits will express itself somehow, whether
in our words, actions, feelings, and/or mental state.

How amazing to think that some mothers are grieving and don't know it.
How amazing to talk about losing one's sense of self and yet not talk about grief.
How amazing that I was grieving, a grief counselor, and didn't recognize it. Me,
well versed in issues of loss and grief, a mother of three, a woman who considers

herself aware and smart, married to an intelligent man who has several degrees himself, including one in psychotherapy. Here I was displaying classic signs of loss and never thought about grief as something I was experiencing relative to my role as a mother. I suppose I was simply trying to survive the onslaught of feelings, new routines, lack of sleep, and the temperamental ways of young children. My attention was so well diverted away from my feelings that I sank deeper into depression and anxiety without questioning their cause. Life with my young children demanded action, not thought. I mean, I would think about the best ways to discipline and entertain my children, how to answer their innumerable questions, how to care for *them* physically, emotionally, and mentally, and perhaps how to use my time most expeditiously, but I didn't ponder my feelings or the reasons for them. With young children in general, time moves in the urgent and immediate, and the pace is ever so challenging. When I did have a moment to be still and indulge a thought for my own, I daydreamed. There seemed to be no need to explore the feelings that I was trying to escape. The workload and drain of caring for my children seemed as great as the love I felt for them; conflicting feelings seemed inevitable and therefore acceptable. The reason sufficed. I was excited, happy, in love, busy, overcome, and captivated because I was a mother. And I was also sad, frustrated, angry, lonely, depressed, and anxious for the same exact reason.

Mothers of all backgrounds in every state around this country share common symptoms and similar experiences of motherhood, and still the connection to grief has not been made obvious to any degree that engenders recognition, acceptance, support, or healing. Symptoms, especially anxiety and depression, are often diagnosed as a medical condition that can be assuaged with the right prescription drugs; this may ease the symptoms but increase the risk of dependence. Further still, drugs are ineffective in actually *healing* any psychological effects of loss, should the issue of loss be relevant. Loss becomes relevant when mothers perceive the numerous changes in their self-esteem, appearance, marital satisfaction, financial status, sexuality, ambitions, etc., as damaging to their sense of self. Loss becomes relevant when mothers feel trapped and desperate, isolated and overwhelmed in a situation that has the power to strip them of self-worth. Loss becomes relevant when a woman's physical, cognitive, social, and emotional responses to motherhood impact her in such a way that she no longer feels familiar to herself. Under these circumstances, grief *must* be acknowledged and treated as a possible (and reasonable) cause for the various symptoms afflicting so many mothers.

Grief is not bias; it does not discriminate. Grief is not an illness or a disorder that has any psychological classification. Grief is not something to conceal, or avoid. Nor is grief a single state of being that can be clearly recognized from one moment to the next. Grief is a function of pain that descends and retreats, moving about as an active process, ever-changing and often camouflaged, but always persistent as an opportunity for growth despite ourselves. In grief we think, feel, and act in ways that are quite different from the ways in which we typically present. Coping skills deteriorate, moods fluctuate, and personalities are shaken. Grief distorts reality in those moments when it hits hard, making the "normal" seem unfamiliar. For mothers, personal and societal expectations and belief systems also factor largely in the experience of grief; that is, how a woman thinks a baby would affect her life, how she thinks she ought to behave and feel after having a baby, and how she thinks of her emotions and their social acceptability.

Dianne shares her experience:

Ted and I were so happy when Elisa was born. I knew I'd be real busy every day, but I guess I expected that I would at least shower and keep myself looking a certain way. A lot of times I didn't either shower or dress better because I started to think that it didn't matter what I looked like as long as the baby was fed and well cared for. I kept the baby in the bathroom with me when I did bathe, but I always felt rushed and unable to complete my usual morning routine, the things I did for myself before the baby came. I guess she needed so much and I wanted to be everything for her that I gave up a lot, never thinking that I would eventually feel miserable about myself. I thought I'd always be happy, playing with her and having lots of fun, but it's definitely not all fun; in fact, most of it isn't. It's a lot of work, for sure, but I keep a smile on my face when we're with other people because I'm afraid of what they might think of me if I dare to complain. I'm supposed to have it all, you know.

Peggy said this about her experience:

I can't tell you how often I sit in the bathroom, the only place I can find in the house to be alone, and cry. I'd say that every time I ask myself, "What's wrong with me?" I cry so much. I know this is supposed to be a good thing, having children and staying home with them, but something is not right here. I have a two-year-old and a three-and-a-half-year-old and I can't believe how hard this is on me. No one knows that I cry this much, not even my husband or mother. Of course I love my children with all my heart, but I still question in my bad moments why I ever planned my children so close. I think in the long run things will work out and I'll be glad they are so close in age, but right now, I'm having a really hard time.

Grief is an expansive topic, and as such I've made three distinctions: the characteristics of grief, the responses to grief, and the symptoms related to grief. These distinctions illuminate the similarities between grief and what mothers describe regarding their experience of motherhood, thus revealing grief as an underlying dynamic. The distinctions also serve to demonstrate the different ways that grief functions in the lives of the mothers who experience it.

Characteristics of Grief

The characteristics of grief depict the general nature of grief in contrast to the more intimate outcries of pain that exist in the other distinctions. For instance, one characteristic of grief is how it "travels." Some authors have described its journey as spiral in movement, rotating upward and slowly away from loss, often passing across the point of origin as it ascends. This description illustrates how feelings related to grief can recur from time to time long after the initial loss. Grief has also been compared to the waves of an ocean; it crashes hard and then retreats until the natural currents bring it back. This characteristic of grief provides temporary relief from the physical and psychological drain of loss. Unlike ocean waves, however, we cannot predict when waves of grief will hit. Grief causes unpredictable, spontaneous emotions.

Joan offers her experience:

I figured that it was hormonal because I seemed to have no control over my emotions. One minute I would be crying and the next minute I would be irate about something, even trivial stuff. I'm only thirty-four years old, but I started thinking that maybe I'm perimenopausal. Just when I concluded that I was nuts, I would feel fine again, happy to be home with the kids and content with life, that is, of course, until something set me off. This [behavior] has gone on for a long time, in and out of these intense moods. It didn't matter if I was weeping or screaming, because either way, I felt miserable and desperate for something, although I don't know what. But I know I wasn't happy in those moments, quite the contrary. I realize that being happy all the time is unrealistic, but these dark places are really dark, if you know what I mean.

Elaine tells her story:

I was a mother at a young age, which may have affected my experience, but so many times throughout my years as a mother I have had these "spells," or so I would tell my husband. During those moments, at different times for different lengths of time, I would have huge doubts about my ability to handle motherhood. Not the work, more like the feeling it [motherhood] gave me. Sometimes I felt happy to be with the kids and other times it felt beyond me, like I was watching someone else raise my kids [because] I didn't feel at all present. Almost like I was afraid to feel the bad feelings and so I shut down. When I explode unexpectedly, which I do more than I'd like to, or just the opposite like withdrawing or being really depressed, it's like all my feelings welled up and couldn't be kept in anymore, and I do what I do to get rid of the feelings or withdraw into my own world for comfort.

Another characteristic of grief is its power to "paralyze" those whom it afflicts. For some individuals, eating, bathing, and socializing are tasks that cannot be accomplished while in the depths of grief. More common are grief-stricken individuals who are so overcome with emotion that they shut down cognitively and/ or emotionally. In this way they are unable to obtain the support and help available to them. In a less demonstrative way, Elaine made reference to this feeling when she said, "I didn't feel at all present." I experienced it as the inability to pick up a phone to call a babysitter or to openly admit to others that I was struggling. I knew I needed help; I needed a reliable babysitter, a social life, a therapist, and some planned alone time. I *knew* what had to happen, I just didn't *do* what had to happen, like pick up a phone and call a therapist or any of the teenagers in my neighborhood who I knew were mature and capable enough to care for my children. But every day my husband would ask if I made the call, and every day I said "no" in a variety of ways and for various reasons. It really is hard to describe this kind of paralysis. I wasn't in denial. I wasn't too shy or uninformed. And once again I wasn't alone in my experience. Several mothers shared the same experience without offering a sound explanation, except that they were generally too tired to act on their own behalf.

Brenda

I don't know why I don't ask for help. I kind of feel stuck in my habits. Every day I wake up and do the same exact things, usually in the same exact order. I thought rou-

tine was supposed to be a good thing [she laughs]. *I guess it's good for kids. For me, it's not so good because nothing ever changes. I go to bed every night exhausted. And I don't look forward to waking up. I don't know how to ask for help or where to find help. Even the thought of looking for help is exhausting. So I just keep going and doing and every night I go to bed exhausted.*

Eileen

I don't know what's the matter with me. I get so mad at myself. My husband has been great. He wants me to do whatever I want. If I want to stay home with the kids, that's great. If I want to go back to work full-time, that would be great too. Whatever I want. And can you believe, I don't know what I want. Sometimes the guilt of leaving them [the children] prevents me from ever making the decision. The guilt, the pressure to do the right thing, to hold up my end of the bargain, to be available for the kids, and funnily enough, I don't think I'm available at all. I'm in this nowhere land of not acting, of not functioning. Days slip by and I realize how lame it is that I can't and don't change the things I know are not right in my life. What is that? What's wrong with me?

I asked Eileen, "Do you think you're just too tired to make big decisions or too tired to be as present for your children as you would like to be?" She said, "I'm tired, of course, aren't all moms? But it's something else, something more, but I can't tell you what that something is, maybe another mom could." After talking a little longer, Eileen said something very interesting. She said that when she's with her children, she's constantly thinking of their safety, constantly looking around for them, constantly listening to a story or a question, and constantly attending to their various needs. She finally said what I was thinking. "You know," she stated, "it's like I'm overloaded. If it's not enough to always be entrenched in their lives, I'm entrenched in the battle to survive it [the overload]. They're so consuming. I guess that's just the way it is when you have kids."

In these words I hear a sense of hopelessness. When something is "just the way it is," life can seem hopeless, and when there's no hope for something different, apathy can take over. Why bother acting if nothing is going to change? I also hear "overload," which was a common word and concept among many mothers I interviewed. Mothers are overloaded with all kinds of stimulation. They are overloaded with the entire experience of motherhood, from the chaos to the tension, from the emotions it arouses in them to the physical demands that are expected of them. Mothers are so "on" all the time with their children that they neglect themselves and become paralyzed to act in ways that would relieve the stimulation. ***Mothers seek to survive overload rather than relieve it.*** In this vein, I remember saying years ago that I was on automatic pilot. The autopilot got the chores done and made sure the kids got their needs met; the autopilot got me through the day. *But the autopilot was the paralyzed state that disabled me!* It prevented me from thinking and acting outside the box, so to speak. My days were programmed to meet certain expectations and responsibilities, which I did. But as programs go, I was limited in how and what I did, even though I was yearning desperately for help and relief.

Mothers also feel paralyzed to act on their own behalf for fear that their need for help signals failure or inadequacies, whether the help is a therapist, a babysitter, or a housecleaning service. No one wants to be thought of or viewed as less capable or less healthy than the next person, and so mothers don't act or speak in any way that would suggest failure. What a scene from the first season of the popular television show *Desperate Housewives* when Lynette, overloaded with the chaos of her kids, runs from the house spewing the words "This is too hard." She leaves her children with Susan and speeds off toward an open soccer field where she is later found by Susan and Bree. Sitting there, Lynette discloses her use of Ritalin and her feelings of failure. "I feel sorry my children have me for a mother. I'm so tired of feeling like a failure. It's so humiliating. Other moms make it look so easy." Susan and Bree are quick to chime in with their shared experience. Lynette ends the scene asking, "Why didn't you ever tell me this?" Susan says, "We think it's easier just to keep it in." And Bree responds, "No one likes to admit they can't handle the pressure." As a final note, Lynette speaks through her tears, "We should tell each other this stuff." Lynette is right. Mothers should tell each other stuff. In not telling, mothers stay stuck in grief, stuck in their personal crisis. In not telling, mothers are further compromised by the shame of not getting the help they know they need, which strikes a blow to their already suffering self-esteem. But *in* telling, mothers might just get the support they need, the advice they want, and a sense of empowerment to change the circumstances that have otherwise kept them grieving.

Perhaps the most poignant characteristic of grief is its ability to cause a person to search for the object that was lost. This impulse to search seems to exist regardless of the type of loss. For instance, a person will search for a lost object, person, or image much in the same way—in an effort to regain or recover what has been "taken." Just as a person will seek to recover his or her lost wallet, bereaved individuals may seek to "find" their deceased loved ones in the design of clouds in the sky or in the vague "presence" standing before them. Similarly, mothers search for lost aspects of themselves when they ask, "What happened to me?" And they seek to find at least something of what they left behind before parenthood. This searching may be in an art class a mother takes out of the blue (like I did), in a makeover, in a continuing education course offered at the community college, or in the Christmas card she personally designs. Likewise, mothers search for meaning in the details of their lives in order to make sense of the loss of self that permeates those same details. With the grace of God, perseverance, journaling, and other modalities, most mothers do find meaning and recover the sense of self that was buried under the workload, sacrifices, and losses related to motherhood.

Dianna shares her thoughts:

My kids are still young and I still have lots to do for them, but I can't help but wonder if there is more I should be doing with my life. I think there is. I get this feeling that I can and should be doing something really important; I just don't know what it is.

I don't think any person would dispute the important role that mothers have in the lives of their children, especially mothers themselves. However, many mothers struggle with the need to fulfill some personal undertaking beyond the one designated to them through childbirth or adoption. I think this is a natural inclination and one that does not replace or undermine the greater task of motherhood. With all due respect to children, spouses, and society, most mothers seek to recover, or find anew, the person within them that wants to be known apart from "mother."

A final note on the characteristics of grief would include defense mechanisms. Defense mechanisms are ways we cope with difficult or intolerable thoughts and feelings. By using defense mechanisms, our unconscious thoughts and feelings are camouflaged or expressed indirectly. Each defense mechanism has its particular purpose, but collectively they provide the opportunity for people to grapple with and slowly incorporate the intensity of an unfamiliar, uncomfortable, sad, or distressing situation. Therefore it would be expected and common for defenses to surge when grief is present. Defense mechanisms do not prevent grief; they merely aid the difficult and painful process of coping with loss. The three most common defense mechanisms associated with grief are idealization, denial, and regression. *Idealization* creates an image of a time, place, or person without flaw. When a person makes use of idealization, he or she recalls a perfect image and not the more realistic account of what truly existed prior to the loss. As a result, the individual may feel more justified in his or her grief and, unfortunately, greater discontent with what the present has to offer.

I idealized my twenties, a time my mind's eye had always been eager to revisit, especially in my thirties when I was adjusting to motherhood. While I reveled in the joys of motherhood for much of the time, I also escaped in the memories of my twenties, a time that allowed me to wander freely and delight in moments with strangers and long walks with close friends. I moved often, traveling abroad and creating change as often as possible. I kept a duffel bag in the trunk of my car ready for the next adventure. It was a decade I remember as all-fulfilling, selfish, and replete with fun; and may I say I wore it well. Motherhood was literally a shock to my system. The duffel bag in my car was replaced with a diaper bag and adventure meant changing a soiled baby at a road stop without the diaper wipes I thought I had put inside the diaper bag! Hardly what I had in mind as adventure only five years earlier. The time had certainly come to settle down, to put into place the nuts and bolts of a family, to be responsible and prepare for new kinds of adventure. The time had come to put aside the rationale for my carefree lifestyle and the phrase (and phase) I defended during most of my twenties, "It's just who I am."

Motherhood seemed to care little about who I was and far more about who I must be. The conflict aroused unbearable tension, and so I dwelled in reveries to escape. I went to perfect places in time, where no care existed and skies were always blue. How could life with temper tantrums and the never-ending needs of young children ever compare to the perfect image my mind created out of the enormous need for relief? It couldn't. I became certain that time before children was the ideal to which I aspired naturally and time spent any other way would sabotage who I really was. I was greatly mistaken. It took me a few years, but I finally realized that I had only pieced together select memories of my twenties and that my twenties had not been perfect after all. The distorted memories served me well by creating an outlet for my tension and a safe haven for the thoughts that soothed my battered spirit. Idealizing my twenties was a coping mechanism I used during a rough period of transition, a transition that temporarily demands focus outside oneself, a time that is not "all about me," unlike my twenties. Daydreaming merely provided the balance I was seeking. Motherhood, especially early motherhood, is a time that speaks of self-sacrifice and attention to those who need their mommies. Idealization only wants to help mommies get through it.

Denial is a defense mechanism that attempts to spare the intensity of loss. During the first few years of motherhood when several losses occur simultaneously (e.g., independence, friendships, physique, free time, spousal intimacy, income, sleep, a quiet meal, personal ambitions), mothers may deny the losses in their lives to avoid the anguish that usually accompanies such profound losses. Often I have wondered if mothers (unconsciously) create additional chaos, such as all their children's extracurricular activities, so that they can blame the chaos for any symptoms and conflicting feelings they experience, thus denying the grief of personal loss. Busy lives don't permit the time to think and feel the ache of loss; denial further ensures that grief doesn't surface and invade the safe space it creates when one feels too vulnerable. In denial, one can at least function and smile without pretense. In denial, one can feel more certain, more steady, and more capable. In denial, one can "honestly" ignore the most important thing about making a big transition, and that is, change often brings losses and gains, and the losses typically create grief.

Regression, the third type of defense mechanism, calls up the "childlike" tendencies we all have from time to time. For instance, a mother might throw a temper tantrum or cry uncontrollably when overwhelmed, much the way a child would act when frustrated or disappointed. To regress is to be out of control, which mothers demonstrate when they feel as though their needs, thoughts, wants, expectations, ideas, etc., are denied or unattainable. Regressive behaviors allow mothers to recoil from a situation that feels threatening to their sense of self; mothers may feel this threat when the demands of childcare result in personal neglect or the demise of personal boundaries (a topic I discuss at greater length in Chapter 6). Whether physical or psychological, personal neglect leads to a diminished sense of self if unattended. Because such a threat exists, mothers may regress as a desperate move to protect their sense of self, recover what they feel is missing, or as a genuine plea for help. In essence, mothers are seeking comfort when they display behaviors that represent an age regression. The comfort may be obtained in different ways, but it generally resides in things that are important, familiar, and fulfilling. What could be more important, familiar, and fulfilling than being in touch with one's sense of self?

Tara shares her feelings:

I literally wanted to crawl into my husband's lap and sit there curled up. I did. I wanted to be held, not hugged, but held and stroked. I asked him to do that only once and it felt great. I didn't want to open my eyes and realize that I was still sitting in my apartment with a colicky three-month-old in the other room who was getting his three-minute nap for the day.

Lisa offers her experience:

I have my share of temper tantrums. I get so frustrated myself that my needs aren't get-ting met. I don't know what I expect my four-year-old to do, but for Pete's sake, when is it my turn for someone to drop everything and let me have my way?

Responses to Grief

Grieving is what people do after a significant loss. Although each individual responds to a particular loss in his or her own way and in his or her own time, lit-erature on grief suggests that most people respond to loss in one or more of the following ways: guilt/shame, anger/resentment, bargaining, fear/anxiety, depres-sion/a sense of failure, helplessness/powerlessness, decreased self-esteem, despair, and ultimately acceptance.

Guilt says, "What have I done?" and "If only …" It reflects responsibility, the claiming of anything that's gone wrong. A bereaved individual feels the burden of what was left unsaid or undone, or perhaps what was said or done prior to the loss of a significant other. In mothers, guilt is apparent in similar reflections. I have asked, "What have I done?" numerous times when recovering from a long day with frustrating toddlers. More guilt followed just having asked the question that communicated regret. Similarly, I know I have said, "If only …" countless times. If only I had waited a few years before having the second baby. If only I had finished school before having children. If only I had a different personality. If only I had taken more time to "find myself" before starting a family. If only I had started a family as a younger woman. My "If only" comments had no rhyme or reason. They were simply irrational impulses blurted out during an intolerable moment of grief, a moment in which everything familiar was out of reach, including my sense of self. A sentence beginning with "If only" is an obvious claim of guilt. When not as obvious, guilt can be found hiding at the root of self-punitive or self-justifying behaviors. Guilt can also be camouflaged by depression, ritualized obsessions, overcompensation, or antagonistic behavior.

Arlene shares her guilt in this story:

Everyone tells me to take care of myself, to get out of the house even if for only a short time. I should do so at least once a day. I know I need the break. I can see changes in me and my moods, like I'm overstretched and ready to snap. Motherhood is hard work, and it's reasonable to want breaks, but usually something happens to prevent me from getting out, and before you know it, it's really late. Day after day this happens and day after day I see myself differently, like I'm not the person I used to be. But it's my fault, I suppose. I have to be stronger and more vocal about my needs and getting help. My husband is willing, I just feel self-conscious about asking him for help after he's been at work all day. There's probably so much I would love to do on my own if given the chance; I'm just not taking the chance.

Samantha writes in an email:

I feel cranky all the time these days. I feel really bad for my kids. I think I'm taking it out on them. I'm always snapping at them for things and being really serious, which I never considered myself to be. I think I have too much going on between the volunteer work that I do for Andrew's class and Girl Scouts, and taking care of the house and all the other little things that add up. I know it's too much. I just don't know how to say no and do less.

Linda's perspective

I gained a lot of weight after I had my son. I let myself go. I hate it, but I don't have the energy or time to work out. I hang out with my son all day and eat when and what he eats. It's a terrible habit. I should stop. I do feel bad about myself and how I look. [Groans] This is harder to talk about than I thought it would be. I guess eating is just as bad as popping pills or drinking because all of them make you feel responsible for your own fate.

I can't help but point out a few things. For instance, Arlene said, "I'm not the person I used to be. But it's my fault, I suppose." Could guilt be any more present than in a comment that claims fault, especially as it relates to personal change? How about her comment that *he's* been at work all day? I'm compelled to note this remark for no other reason than to highlight its absurdity. Arlene needs to understand that she's been at work all day as well. Finally, "I'm just not taking the chance" reflects Arlene's guilt for not pursuing the opportunities that would allow her to fully actualize her potential. In Samantha's letter, she exposes the guilt she feels for "snapping at [the kids]" because she is overwhelmed with what she has taken on as her responsibility. Mothers often have feelings of guilt when they recognize how their moods affect their children. Finally, Brenda's words "I let myself go" and "I should stop" capture the essence of this book, this chapter, and my discussion on guilt, and so I needn't say more except for two things. One is that guilt and feeling responsible for loss go hand in hand, as in "I let it happen." And two, when embarrassment enters guilt, it becomes *shame*.

Anger is considered a staple in grief. In nearly all theories, there is a place for anger. Anger cries out blame and looks to others as the cause of pain. Anger is a complex emotion that is likely to be displaced and easy for others to avoid, since it takes on such a personal quality. Anger pushes others away at a time when the grieving individual needs support and understanding. Mothers who are frequently or easily irritated are likely to be struggling with the losses inherent to motherhood, barring no other life event of equal or greater magnitude that could be causing the anger. The anger may be blatant, it may be subtle or even dormant, it may be well disguised or completely misdirected, but anger usually surfaces periodically throughout times of grief. ***Anger is perhaps the most normal of all responses to grief because it protests separation.***** For example, a bereaved woman expresses anger because her loved one has died and will not return; a mother expresses anger because some aspect of her life or her self has vanished. Although these are different circumstances, each woman is protesting separation—separation from another and separation from self, respectively. In the latter example, the anger a mother exhibits may be drawing its strength from the daily frustrations of not having her personal needs satisfied (e.g., quiet time, time for a hobby), which leads to the deterioration of self; likewise, the *resentments* that develop from unfilled needs and unrecognized grief may create the expression of anger. Of course, one could argue for a less threatening explanation that the anger a mother displays is simply the knee-jerk response to a child who has pushed the wrong buttons too many times. However, when the anger is intense, expressed often, or in combination with other symptoms, chances are that the anger signals a great need that is unfulfilled, whether that need is to unite with a deceased loved one or to embrace one's sense of self and the aspects of life that ground that self.

Bargaining begs mercy. "If I do this, will you give me that?" Often terminally ill patients will make promises to God so that God in turn will spare them the inevitability intrinsic to a terminal illness. Likewise, bereaved individuals often pray as a means of receiving comfort during their time of distress. Mothers, on the other hand, seek their comfort or "recovery" in slightly different ways. For example, they bargain money for time when they hire a babysitter or when they register their children for preschool. Although there are great benefits to having children in preschool, mothers have admitted that preschool serves them equally as well. When a young child is in school for a few hours, Mom has time to rest, Mom has time to do what's needed to finish a long overdue project or to hear a thought, uninterrupted. Time allows the pursuit of ambitions and the chance to remember, experience, and embrace all things familiar. Time alone becomes the most sought after, the most quintessential space for mothers to recover from the strain of motherhood.

Fear is another response to grief. It looks, feels, and sounds like anxiety but it's not. Anxiety is covered in depth in the following chapter because it plays such a large and distinguished role in grief. As for fear, it exists in response to grief primarily as a reaction to the intensity of emotions that often erupt after something of great value has been lost. The intensity of any emotion can be frightening, especially when compounded by the already existing duress of loss or when such intense emotions have rarely been experienced. When a mother tells me, "I don't know who I am anymore," I hear the kind of fear that might exist in a young child lost at an amusement park. With lights glaring, rides moving, and music playing, it's a place that holds great promise for a good time unless a child is there alone among hundreds, frightened without the one familiar face that the child knows, needs, and trusts. And so the child, with fear governing his or her actions, cries, runs, and seeks to find that one familiar face that provides the child with a sense of safety and wholeness. Under the same circumstances, another child may feel overcome with a sense of *helplessness*. Standing alone in the park, the child freezes, not knowing how to bring about the familiar face and the sense of wholeness that he or she has lost. When separated from those we love or separated from things familiar, many people become frightened or *powerless* to act. Similarly, the huge transition into motherhood can elicit feelings of uncertainty and fear because it is a change from what has been known to something unknown. When these changes extend beyond chores and schedules and impact personality, thoughts, and behavior, fear can become part of a mother's experience. Motherhood holds great promise for a good time, but without the sense of self mothers depend on for comfort, they may undoubtedly experience fear.

Depression is not solely expressed by sadness or feeling blue; depression goes beyond sadness. Depression prevents the engaging of activities that used to be pleasurable; depression limits motivation and/or energy for what was once energizing or fun. Depression affects the way a mother feels about herself, how she eats and sleeps, and how she thinks about others and life events. Likewise, depression may cause a mother to think in terms of "poor me," a victim of circumstance who feels deprived or who broods about the future or a past that is out of reach. A depressed mother may exhibit poorer personal hygiene that can be observed in such tendencies as not changing her clothes daily and neglecting basic grooming habits. Symptoms of depression may also include sadness that lasts longer than two weeks; feelings of worthlessness, hopelessness, and pessimism; thoughts of death or suicide; self-reproach; extreme fatigue; loneliness; restlessness; and vulnerability. Researchers estimate that of the 7 million women who suffer with clinical depression, only one in three women with depression are properly diagnosed (WebMD). Other data claims that one in four women suffer from depression with up to **50 percent** of depression in women going **unrecognized**. Furthermore, research supports the finding that depression affects more women than men, perhaps because of the combined effects of biological, genetic, and social factors. The World Health Organization declares depression as the number one disease affecting women. However, I found no statistic on how many of these women are mothers, except for data on postpartum.

Despair perceives the future as dark, so dark that death is often sought as relief. Despair typically makes a person lethargic and quiet, inconspicuous and aimless. On occasion, despair can erupt into rage in its last attempt to fight what is perceived as a losing battle. The face of despair lacks life and hope.

Elizabeth

I remember thinking that it was all downhill from here. I had graduated from an Ivy League school, a goal I had set for myself, and now there was nothing more to achieve. I was home all the time with my two kids, two very strong-willed kids at that. One day we were outside in the garage getting ready to play in the snow. It was such hard work getting boots and gloves on, fighting for the hats to be put on their heads. And I knew all along that they'd be done playing in less time than it would take me to get them ready. I could feel the tension building inside of me. I was getting frustrated because they weren't listening to me. I finally blew. I was raging. I just lost it. My husband came home right at that moment. He was angry with me for being so out of control. He made some comment that I was a failure as a mother. Minutes later I was upstairs, alone in my bedroom. I remember the feeling vividly. I must have felt despair because I was thinking that suicide was my only way out. I was in a place where I couldn't think of any good times with my kids, only all the work, sacrifice, and the constant expectations of me. There just seemed like this dark future at that moment. Suicide was my only thought of how to get away. I couldn't think of any other way to fix things, to make myself happy in this situation. It must be despair when you can't even think to do anything but kill yourself.

Elizabeth and I talked at great length about that day in her life. She admitted that she has a history of clinical depression, but she never experienced rage in all the years she suffered from depression. Her feelings of rage only evidenced after she had her children. Likewise she had never experienced despair or feelings of suicide as she did in her room that winter's day. When I asked her why she may have had those thoughts, she said, "It was building up inside of me for a long time. You know, you have children and you are expected to handle any and all of the situations that arise. You have your children, love them, and enjoy them. But it takes a lot of work, all the time and a lot of patience and sacrifice all the time. I had reached a point where I felt as though all of me had been sacrificed. There was nothing of me left. I felt trapped in that moment and so incredibly *hopeless* about things changing. Things had gotten so bad. I was miserable. I never wanted to leave my room." Fortunately Elizabeth reached out for help. Her clinical depression was of course a great contributing factor in the way she had been feeling, and so the right medications went a long way in helping her manage her moods. However, "all of me had been sacrificed" highlights the need for intervention beyond medication. These words and the feelings attached to them represent loss of self (and grief) to the utmost degree.

Acceptance is the response to grief after all other possible responses have had their chance to be heard. Accepting loss is to reconcile with change, change that once caused pain. To accept a loss is to speak, think, see, hear, and remember without the genuine pain that a fresh loss incites. A bereaved individual can look at a picture or hear a story of a deceased loved one without "falling apart." He or she can actually smile for all things missed even if a tear falls. Mothers can reminisce about days gone by without resenting the work, challenges, and sacrifices of the present. I can think about my twenties and remember how I lived and what I did during that decade without the urge to put the duffel bag back into my car and drive away, alone. ***Recognizing the many changes in my life as lost pieces of my self proved necessary in order for me to accept my new role and the lifestyle that went along with it.*** Just as it's easy to love one's child, it's easy to welcome all the wonders and joys that a child adds to life. The difficult part is to *accept the possibility* that being a mother can sometimes hurt the woman inside.

Symptoms Related to Grief

No two people will share the exact same journey through the pain of loss. The symptoms of grief can range in intensity from mild to severe and endure from days to years. As for kind, symptoms of grief can be categorized as physical, emotional/psychological, cognitive, and social/behavioral. Mothers who are grieving their loss of self may experience any number of these symptoms in any combination at any time. Of all the symptoms, crying is one of the most obvious signs of feeling overwhelmed with sadness, frustration, or despair. I cried often and usually alone, although there were many times when the tears came streaming out unexpectedly while in conversation with my husband, mother, sister, or best friend. In those moments I remember feeling embarrassed, as though the tears exposed me as the failure I thought myself to be. Certainly it spoke of weakness, insecurity, and misery, I figured. Worse than any of this, though, was that I knew I wouldn't get the kind of help that I was desperately seeking. I wanted to be saved. I wanted someone to reach into my life and pull me out. Because this was not likely to happen, nor did I really want to leave, I cried to relieve the tension I felt when I couldn't find what I had been (unknowingly) searching for at home. I was searching for me.

My tears were only one manifestation of the loss of self and the associated grief that I experienced at that time in my life. Here's a look at more symptoms of grief that mothers may experience, from the most obvious to the most obscure.

Physical Symptoms

- fatigue, restlessness/overactivity
- stress-related illnesses (e.g., thyroid disease/Graves' disease, MS, irritable bowel syndrome)
- a general decline in health (stomach/intestinal problems, high blood pressure, asthma, GERD)
- sleeping problems (e.g., night waking, insomnia)
- muscle tension (headaches, backaches, etc.)
- tightness in the throat or chest
- decrease or increase of appetite (weight loss/gain)
- low energy, palpitations, oversensitivity to noise

Emotional/Psychological Symptoms

- irritability/lowered tolerance, anger
- depression, anxiety
- sadness (e.g., abrupt or prolonged bouts of crying)
- loss of identity, sudden changes in mood (mood swings), self-doubt
- irrational fears, self-consciousness

- decreased self-esteem
- lack of self-concern
- a feeling of losing one's mind
- preoccupation with a former reality
- denial, regression, and other defense mechanisms
- guilt/shame, resentment
- a sense of failure or fear of failure
- despair, feelings of helplessness

Cognitive Symptoms

- absentmindedness, difficulty concentrating or remembering
- disorganization (e.g., starting one task and leaving it unfinished to start another task)
- impaired decision-making and intellectual processing
- negative internal dialogue (self-talk)
- distorted perceptions of self and others

Social/Behavioral Symptoms

- withdrawal/avoidance of others, loneliness, isolation
- withdrawal from normal activity or activities that previously held great interest
- a strain in relationships
- sexual difficulties (e.g., performance, desire, and intimacy)
- increased use of nicotine, alcohol, or other drugs
- chemical addiction relapse
- excessive use of television as a means of escaping
- difficulty having fun with family or friends
- the interruption of usual patterns of behavior

Since most of these symptoms are self-explanatory, mothers need only to consider each category of symptoms as they relate to their lives and determine for themselves if parallels exist between how they feel, act, and think and the symptoms of grief listed here. In closing this chapter, I wish for the reader to keep in mind two things: Not every symptom of grief will present in every grieving individual; we all grieve with different symptoms, in different time frames, and with varying intensities. Second, and perhaps more important, is the understanding that ***women can be good, loving, and devoted mothers while grieving the losses they perceive in their lives and in themselves***. I've discovered through interviews and personal experience that mothers usually remain physically and emotionally available to their children *in spite of* the grief that occasionally distracts them. Grief is powerful, but it seems as though motherhood is more powerful; not even grief can stand between a mother and her child. Mothers may cry, scream, forget to make dinner, or demand alone time, but mothers stay. Mothers stay to care for and love their children in the many ways it means to love. When one grieves, one does not forget to love; in fact, love is most profound in grief because, ironically, despite its dark nature, grief sheds light on what's most important in life. And so, yes, I grieved for the sense of self I lost in all the tasks and changes associated with motherhood, but I look at my children today and feel proud of who they've become and my role in that process. I can say without a moment's hesitation that I was and continue to be a good mom.

FOUR:
MATERNAL INTRAPERSONAL ANXIETY: WHY ANXIETY AND WHERE IT BEGINS

o o o o o o o o o o o o o o o o o o o o o o o o o o o o o o o o o o

"Where did I go?" Perhaps an equally challenging and imposing question is, "Did anyone notice that I left?" I'm aware that after weeks, months, and years of being a mother and losing my sense of self, I am less inclined to talk about it as if I couldn't explain it if I tried or that no one would understand my choice of words should I explain. Worse yet, maybe no one would care. I feel cursed that I even think about these things. I actually think about the person I was, the "me" that would sit amidst the dry autumn leaves and stare at an ant, empathizing with its struggle to carry the crumb from here to there. Wasteful times that allowed me to hear my internal voice, the nonsensical and the serious. As motherhood has grown on me, I hear my voice less and less. Rather I hear the sounds of children and their needs. I hear the calls of responsibility, the words of direction as I prioritize the tasks to be accomplished each day. I hear the chatter of the TV and the call to be my husband's partner. The voice persists as the familiarity fades. And with it my sense of self, a self I love. How strange to come to a place where I hear the voice say, "I miss you."

—Diary entry, Spring 2000

Why Anxiety

I wrote that entry while sitting in my Advanced Social Work Practice course at Rutgers University during my final semester. My apologies to Professor Lowenstein for not paying more attention to him; I suppose the entry couldn't wait. Weaved throughout my notebook are similar entries, each describing some set of feelings I had about motherhood or the loss of self that I was experiencing. Interestingly, I never once used the word "anxiety," and yet anxiety is considered fundamental among most grief theories, either as a symptom of grief (one emotion of many in response to loss) or as *the* core emotion central to grief (the collective experience); that is, grief *is* anxiety. As I mentioned in the Introduction, the pastoral theologian David Switzer wrote in detail about the collective experience of grief in a theory called Grief as a function of Separation Anxiety. From this theoretical perspective, anxiety is the core experience of an infant when separated from the mothering figure; the word "grief" is used to specify the anxiety experienced during the separation. Since no mother can be with her child 100 percent of the time, it's theorized that an infant learns of anxiety through his or her initial experiences of separation from the mother or mothering figure.

While infants don't have the intellectual ability to understand the meaning of helplessness, abandonment, and the other consequences of separation, infants do respond to pleasure and pain, comfort and discomfort. For instance, when an infant's needs are not met, a sense of discomfort, displeasure, and pain mount, which cause the infant to cry. If the needs continue to be unmet, the infant will eventually display what might be described as panic. When the infant is finally soothed with comfort and pleasure (i.e., food, warmth, or physical touch), the panic is relieved and the crying generally stops. In this repeated experience, an infant *learns* to equate the presence of the mothering figure with the satisfaction of needs in contrast to the absence (separation) of the mothering figure, which arouses discomfort, frustration, pain, and panic. It's the dissonance between pain and pleasure, comfort and discomfort that creates the learning of anxiety; anxiety is the expression of pain when a threat of separation (a threat to the integrity of the self) is perceived. That is, separation is the impetus for anxiety.

Infants, no doubt, become adults, and as they do they seek significant relationships that continue to fulfill their physical and emotional needs for comfort (e.g., touch, affection, warmth, love). Adults typically establish many significant relationships over the course of a lifetime. When any of these relationships are lost, the loss stimulates the learned response to separation from the mothering figure (the first state of anxiety), thus creating anxiety in the adult confronted with the present loss of an emotionally significant other. In other words, when an adult experiences loss, it reactivates the anxiety (pain) of separation learned in early infancy. So what the adult knows, describes, and feels as grief is actually anxiety. Anxiety is grief, and it is aroused because the adult's sense of self feels threatened or jeopardized by the separation that occurs by way of loss. The external event of loss through death, divorce, or a broken relationship prompts the awareness of this threat.

Maternal Intrapersonal Anxiety (MIA) differs radically from this theory in that it is not the loss of a significant other that poses a threat to the self and creates anxiety, but rather it's the loss of one's sense of self that creates anxiety. For many mothers the perceived loss of physique, personality traits (e.g., humor), sexuality, financial status, lifestyle, relationships, self-esteem, etc., impacts their sense of self to the degree that the actual integrity of their "self" is threatened. *This threat to the integrity of the self, this cause for anxiety, is what many mothers know, describe, and feel but rarely if ever recognize or acknowledge as grief.* Freud wrote, "Mourning is regularly the reaction to the loss of a loved person, or to the loss of some abstraction which has taken the place of one." In MIA, a mother's sense of self is the abstraction, and the lost sense of self is what takes the place of a lost loved one. The well-being generated by a healthy sense of self represents value similar to the value one imparts to a significant other. To lose (or become separated from) something of value will cause a person to grieve, whether the value exists in the emotional attachment that occurs in interpersonal relationships, or in an abstract notion of self that contributes to a person's overall sense of well-being. The concepts of value and separation are central to both grief theory and MIA.

Where It Begins: A Boundary Issue

When a person is separated from something of value, he or she will grieve. For mothers experiencing MIA, grief results because they are "separated" from the ideals, needs, dreams, self-image, friendships, confidence, general personality, etc., that contributed to the identity and sense of self they knew prior to children. In other words, mothers grieve because they lose their sense of self. Said in yet another way, mothers grieve because they lose their personal boundaries. Let me elaborate. Somewhere along the way, most people develop personal boundaries. A boundary is a limit, so to speak, a line we figuratively construct to show others where our comfort zone begins and ends. Personal space is one of the most obvious boundaries we create. Doesn't it feel uncomfortable when someone stands too close while engaging you in conversation? It does for most people, and so they generally react by taking a step back and away. But there's more to boundaries than personal space and reactions far more complicated than physically stepping back.

In some great way, boundaries define us. Boundaries involve our feelings, needs, desires, values, thoughts, decisions, hopes, dreams, and intuitions. Boundaries reflect the inner workings of the "self" we claim by representing what is important to us. For example, I love alone time. I *need* a certain amount of alone time. Time alone invigorates me and allows me the opportunity to rejuvenate and access the peace I have yet to find any other way. This particular boundary was often violated by others who felt that they consistently needed or wanted me present. And I, feeling overly responsible and weak, allowed this boundary to be violated. However, this acquiescence led to despair and grief because it slowly chipped away at a major boundary at the core of my inner being. My sense of self deteriorated a little bit in every occasion I neglected myself and allowed others to take from me when I was not prepared to give physically, emotionally, mentally, or otherwise.

Kim shares her story:

My daughter is so clingy. She always was. Now she is seven and still she is always pulling at my body or hanging on me. It's uncomfortable. And then when my son does the same thing, probably more in a playful way, it's too much. I just want to shake them off me. It's too close. It's confining. That kind of energy along with their giddiness makes my body tighten. [Pause] *I get irritable pretty quickly with that kind of stuff.*

Healthy boundaries protect the self and set limits on the behaviors of others. Healthy boundaries allow a mother's sense of self to thrive because her needs, desires, dreams, etc., are being honored when fulfilled and protected from those who attempt to sabotage that sense of self. Unfortunately, however, having healthy boundaries around youngsters is a task too tall for many mothers. Many mothers sacrifice (willingly or not, consciously or not) the boundaries necessary for things such as strong self-esteem, intimacy, independence, and overall well-being. Although it's quite natural that boundaries blur when falling in love, whether with another adult or with one's child (see M. Scott Peck, *The Road Less Traveled*), mothers ignore or put aside what they need, want, dream, expect, value, feel, etc., because they are frequently striving to please, quiet, avoid, or satisfy (e.g., satisfy the needs of others, avoid toddler tantrums, quiet a persistent child, or please a spouse).

In meeting the challenge and responsibilities akin to parenting, mothers often betray the self within them that begs for attention. Neglect leads to deterioration, and before you know it, a mother's sense of self is gone and symptoms appear, symptoms related to grief. Boundaries are therefore necessary, particularly for mothers of young children because young children don't appreciate boundaries. They don't know boundaries, they don't like boundaries, and they especially don't want their mothers to have boundaries. However, mothers need boundaries. This is not to suggest that mothers should neglect their children. Rather, I am suggesting that mothers listen to what *they* need, dream, expect, desire, value, etc., and nurture those boundaries that secure the sense of self that is reflected in what they hear. They must balance what others want and need with what they want and need. Understandably a delicate balance, but when the scale becomes *consistently* lopsided, mothers suffer. Without boundaries, mothers cannot have a strong or healthy sense of self.

The most useful boundaries are flexible yet assertive. Having flexible boundaries allows mothers to participate actively in their lives as opposed to passively allowing life (and life circumstances) to happen to them. When children need and demand their mothers to the point where mothers feel overwhelmed and desperate, I find it safe to say that boundaries are being violated. Physical, mental, and emotional boundaries can be violated daily in a mother's life. For instance, when a mother's energy is drained to the point where she neglects her appearance and health, a physical boundary is violated. When a mother doesn't have space to call her own or when noise and chaos consume her, her physical boundaries are violated; when physical closeness between husband and wife breaks down, a physical boundary is dishonored (i.e., if the partners desire the physical closeness and don't get it). Likewise when mothers do not receive the privacy they seek when using the bathroom, getting dressed, or speaking on the telephone (thanks to their children), physical boundaries are once again violated. Although these may seem inconsequential and perfectly normal in the context of life with young children, they can seriously affect mothers when viewed along with the emotional and mental boundaries that tend to be easily and consistently violated as well.

Examples of mental and emotional boundaries include personal preferences, wishes, goals, and needs, such as the need for alone time, the need to pursue a personal ambition, the need to develop and nurture friendships, the need for attention/intimacy/love, and the need to have a few uninterrupted thoughts. Mental and emotional boundaries are wide-ranging and imperative to satisfy (even if occasionally) in the scope of what it takes to have and maintain a healthy sense of self. When ignored, disregarded, denied, or limited by anyone, boundaries falter and a mother's sense of self slips away along with her overall health, which shows up in her various symptoms, conflicting feelings, and negative internal dialogue. The point is that when personal boundaries dissolve, so too does a mother's sense of self, which leads to grief and the experience of MIA. MIA is the grief that corresponds to a lost sense of self, whether that sense of self deteriorates through a perception of change or in the violation of personal boundaries (often one and the same).

A violation of a mental or emotional boundary may sound like this, "You shouldn't feel that way" or any remark that uses the word "should," as in you should feel, think, want, choose, believe, decide, etc. I know in my own life I have often heard that I should, and as much as I may have agreed or even acted on that should, it usually felt uncomfortable in a way that spoke volumes; a personal boundary was being violated. I also think we violate our own boundaries when we avoid confronting others, neglect to share our true feelings, accept blame unnecessarily, or permit unjust criticism. During many of my interviews, women described how they had been criticized by their spouses, in-laws, children, friends, and family on topics ranging from domestic abilities to sexuality and appearance. It seems that others don't hesitate to verbalize their opinions on how women "perform" in their role as mothers. And unfortunately, many mothers tolerate it and even buy into it. But make no mistake about it, unsolicited opinions, especially hurtful opinions, are invasions of personal boundaries and cause mothers to move deeper into their loss of self and the experience of MIA. MIA is a state of being that harbors the manifestations of grief.

Call it grief, call it anxiety, it doesn't really matter as long as we as a society recognize that something is happening to mothers everywhere. Mothers feel it and exhibit the signs and symptoms associated with it. Because the signs and symptoms tend to come and go, we don't usually consider grief as an explanation or a cause. However, when viewed in the context of grief, sporadic symptoms make perfect sense (see characteristics of grief in Chapter 3). What doesn't make sense is how grief has escaped the explanation of mothers' angst for so many years. Perhaps it's because society in general barely knows what to do with grief. The truth is, grief makes most people uncomfortable. They don't know what to say, and when they do say something, it is generally void of sound advice or insight. For example, how many of us have heard comments like "Time heals all wounds," "He lived a good life," "What doesn't break us only makes us stronger," or "You could always get *another* dog." Shamefully I admit that it was I who suggested another dog to a grieving acquaintance who had recently experienced the loss of her beloved pet. I couldn't believe the words came out of my mouth. I didn't intend to insult this woman or undermine her grief, but I did. So there you have it, grief counselors can say stupid things too in awkward and uncomfortable moments. Grief rattles most people, and unfortunately, most people want to sidestep the emotional upheaval of loss and disregard the simple empathy that grieving individuals seek after losing something of great value. Loss is not intended to elicit an intellectual response but rather an emotional response. Loss hurts and should be addressed in the emotional context in which it belongs, otherwise grieving individuals may deny, disguise, repress, or shortchange their grief.

Mothers tend to intellectualize their feelings. Not once in the time I spent with mothers did I hear the simple truth, "I miss my friends, I miss my waistline, I miss my sex life, I miss my freedom, and I miss my financial independence. I miss my self-esteem and my sense of worth. I miss these things and it hurts so gosh darn bad." My interviews reveal that mothers are more likely to say either directly or indirectly, "What's wrong with me?" This question addresses the intellect, as if seeking a rational answer to what is often an emotionally driven experience. Mothers rarely make a connection between their feelings and the occurrence of loss; far more often they connect the strain of motherhood with their emotional and physical state. In essence they deny their grief. They push their feelings away, develop symptoms, and maintain the busy schedules that keep them distant from the grief that may exist. Unfortunately, when mothers slight the enormous impact of motherhood and the changes that may be perceived as losses, they become vulnerable to many feelings—feelings that reflect anxiety. MIA identifies this anxiety as the culmination of the many symptoms associated with the grief in loss that goes unrecognized and unresolved.

Allison (mother of two) shares her feelings:

I feel bad all the time, or so it seems. I'm always tired and down. I just want to go away from everything, be by myself. At first I thought it was only because it was winter, cold and dreary. We had to stay indoors on most days and that can be depressing, I guess. Being indoors so much kept me extremely accessible. It was exhausting. But I'm still so down. It's like I'm looking for the reason why I feel so sh____y. And then I feel even worse when I complain, so I don't anymore. I'm just hoping it passes, soon. I want to be happy. I love my kids, but they take a lot out of me.

It's no wonder mothers resist grief and rarely admit to feeling bad. The society in which they live resists grief. Who in their right mind wants to ride against the tide of the society in which they live? However, society does more than resist grief. Society esteems what mothers are typically not. Society esteems wealth, independence, power, success, beauty, intelligence, sex appeal, and health. Mothers often contradict what is held up as valuable despite the occasional stroking they get from the politically correct due that is owed them. Let's face it, most mothers with young children wear clothes that are comfortable and expendable and they choose convenience over style most days of the week; they spend more of their time engaged in mother and child related activities than any other type of social event, leaving them to feel intellectually starved or "fragile." I once used the word "super-de-duper" (from *Barney*) when conversing with a professor from my master's program. Red as a beet and as self-conscious as can be, I shrugged off the awkward moment in the only way I knew how to, with humor and the unpretentious manner of a humble, hardworking, and devoted mom.

Mothers also sacrifice some or all of their income potential while they are at home with the children, leaving them financially dependent on other sources or on a spouse. According to Ann Crittenden, author of *The Price of Motherhood*, one-quarter of the wives in American families with children at home earn nothing; that is, they are completely dependent on a partner. Likewise, mothers don't generally feel "powerful" or healthy. While interviewing I discovered that many mothers feel as though their opinions are not taken as seriously as women in the workforce, their presence and "stories" are less appreciated (e.g., when at social gatherings), and their time is not valued. In terms of health, most mothers laid claim to at least three or more symptoms, making them feel far less healthy than at any other time in their lives.

Lisa D. (mother of twin three-year-old boys) describes herself:

I think of myself as a good person. I try really hard to do a good job with the boys and the house, but it's hard when you feel so terrible all the time. I suffer with migraines and chronic fatigue. I also have trouble sleeping, which causes me to wake up tired and usually irritable. I'm involved in lots of play activities for them, but that's hard too because of the headaches and backaches. I sound like a mess, don't I? I don't remember feeling like this five years ago.

Corrie shares this story:

Every once in a while I get together with old friends from work. I don't do it as often because our worlds have become so different. It's like I don't get them and they don't get me. They don't have a clue what my life is like even when I try to explain. It doesn't matter really. I just think they think I don't have much going on worth talking about. And I guess in the scope of great conversation, I don't have much to say. My world became very small when Ryan came along. I rarely watch the news and hardly ever listen to my kind of music. In the car it's usually kiddie songs. It's all right with me. It is what it is, for now.

Melissa's story

Before I had my first child, I did daydream about all the fun and pleasure I would experience after the baby came. I had been married six years already and was comfortable in my life. My husband and I were ready and excited about becoming parents. Once the baby came, I knew I would be nursing through the nights and adjusting my schedule to care for the baby. I planned it all out. Once the baby came, we had a blast, really. We slept with her and had many moments when we didn't know what to do, but we were all right. Then somewhere along the way, things changed, or I changed, I'm not sure. It was almost like the "honeymoon" was over. There was so much work to do, and I realized how little time I had for me and my friends or anything that I used to do. I wasn't even able to finish one conversation with a friend on the phone. These kinds of things really started to bother me. I don't know if I would have called it anxiety at the time, but I guess I didn't know how to handle the demands of a child while taking care of myself. I was really happy that I had my baby, and we were even talking about a second [child], but deep down, I was off. I wasn't myself. It's like I had a perpetual knot in my stomach that I couldn't get rid of.

I asked Melissa what the knot would say if it had a voice of its own, and she responded, "I don't like what's happening. I want a lot of things to be the way they used to be, especially me, and I'm afraid it's only going to get worse." Pushing a little harder, I asked what she meant by "it" when she said "it's only going to get worse." Melissa said, "Me, my feelings. I don't feel like I'm in my own skin anymore. I've become Mommy and very little else."

When MIA Remains Unrecognized and Unattended

MIA (that is, grief) may exist to the degree that a mother's physical and psychological functioning is disrupted. When left unattended, grief may emerge in unexpected and counterproductive ways. Perhaps the most serious consequence of unattended grief exists in the potential for physical disease. I have read numerous articles from various sources that suggest that stress (including the stress associated with grief) and lowered immune function are interrelated. With lowered immune function, mothers are susceptible to such maladies as chronic colds, colitis, thyroid disease (which I have), irritable bowel syndrome, asthma, gout, multiple sclerosis, fibromyalgia, chronic fatigue syndrome, lupus, and chronic indigestion. In fact, this is only a sampling of medical conditions that mothers offered during my interviews. I am not suggesting that unrecognized and unattended grief *caused* these medical conditions, but rather that the subliminal stress in unattended grief be *considered* as a contributing factor involved in their onset.

The physical ramifications of grief that may present for mothers when their grief remains unattended include sudden or intense bouts of crying, fatigue, lack of motivation, restlessness, weight gain or weight loss, sleep disturbances, heart palpitations, irritability, nervousness, decreased energy, and lack of sexual desire. The social consequence of unattended grief in mothers may evidence in behaviors that are uncharacteristic of the mother harboring the grief. For example, some mothers might become over-involved with others, almost clingy as if to avoid being alone to experience the angst of their grief. In contrast, other mothers might show little or no interest in the activities that used to excite them. They might be less focused when engaged in conversation or withdrew from close friends and family, even their own children.

Lauren (as described by a friend)

Lauren is one of the nicest people you'll ever meet. When I met her several years ago she was dynamic, always dressed to kill, and busy with work. I mean, she always looked terrific. Her hair was always done so nicely and her makeup always impeccable. You got the feeling that she never had to work too hard at looking that good. Yes, she was the envy of us moms. In any case, she had her first child close to four years ago and a second came shortly thereafter. Just this past year, she had a third. But we rarely see Lauren now. It seems like over the years she became less social. I would see her from time to time walking the kids through the neighborhood, but she didn't stop to talk as she used to do. At first I thought maybe I had done something to upset her, but after talking to the other neighborhood women, her friends, I realized it wasn't me but her. Some of her other friends worry about her. They say she's just not herself. She doesn't look good or sound good. When she has stopped to talk, I was told that she sounded depressed; she missed work but wasn't sure what to do with the children should she return to work. She also mentioned that she felt trapped. That's exactly how she looks, like a woman who is so overwhelmed that she's given up. I feel bad for her.

Unrecognized or unresolved grief may also emerge in various psychological ways that range from depression to despair, from guilt to anger, and from low-ered self-esteem to helplessness. Mothers are affected differently by each of these emotions, and each emotion can play out differently in every mother; however, all these emotions may relate directly to unattended grief. The cognitive ramifica-tions of unattended grief show up mostly in negative internal dialogues. Negative internal dialogues are private displays of grief, known to no one but the person who speaks the words in silence. Mothers in grief usually have internal dialogues that suggest loss, although mothers generally miss the meaning in their words and only hear how they are failing as mothers. This expression of unattended grief may affect mothers and their children in the most profound yet subtle way. For example, a private thought such as "I can't do anything right" influences nearly everything a mother does; and, of course, children model nearly everything their mothers do and how they do it.

Last but certainly not least, unattended grief may beset mothers spiritually (or for some, philosophically). When a mother unknowingly grieves a lost sense of self, she cannot possibly resolve any conflicts surrounding that grief. One conflict that naturally evolves from a lost sense of self is the search for meaning. This con-flict says, "I'm lost but I have to find myself in a new self-image, in a new mean-ing for my self." In not creating a new image of self, a woman perpetuates the natural search for meaning around the crisis that exists in losing a well-established pre-child identity. For instance, my pre-child identity incorporated a sense of confidence, leisure, freedom, financial independence, etc., that I did not possess in my life as a new mother who chose to stay at home with her children. I felt awkward and unprepared for many of the tasks related to childcare. I also felt less attractive and less esteemed. As a stay-at-home mom, I couldn't shirk my respon-sibilities at whim (as I did prior to children), and I didn't believe I could establish financial security of my own. Motherhood had jolted my former identity (or sense of self) to the point where it collapsed. My feelings, symptoms, and negative self-talk conveyed my response to this (intra) personal catastrophe. It was only through time, grief work, new boundaries, and discipline that I rediscovered those aspects of my self that were important to me; I incorporated those aspects into a new image of my self, a self that included (and embraced) the many changes in my life that reflect the fact that I am a mother.

Becoming a mother triggers many changes for women, changes that often involve a sense of loss. Since these losses are not generally viewed as legitimate or worthy of being grieved, mothers often overlook the possibility of grief playing a part in their many feelings, thoughts, and symptoms. From my perspective as a mother, interviewer, and professional social worker, I understand how mothers may think it's easier to deny their feelings and suffer silently rather than risk being judged or criticized for having what others might consider uncommon or unnatural reactions to motherhood. That is, I understand why mothers often wear what author Susan Maushart termed "the mask of motherhood." On the other hand, I think it's time for the mask of motherhood to reveal itself as the grief inherent in one of the most powerful and transforming periods of a woman's life. This book and my construct of MIA attempt to do just that. Once revealed, it is my hope that mothers accept their feelings with less judgment and move closer to the place of personal growth and rediscovery that awaits them. In doing so, they may find the sense of self that holds the health and happiness they seek.

FIVE:
THE RIPPLE EFFECT

I am forever awed by the impact I have on my children and their behavior. I remember one particular day when this truth hit me like no other day. I was getting ready to go out for the evening with my husband. He was not home yet; I was alone with the three kids. As you can probably guess, the children were following me around the house. As I was feeling the pressure to be ready on time, I was becoming more irritable. Sensing this irritability, my son Daniel cried to be picked up and coddled, which of course was the last thing I felt like doing, and so I didn't. In response, Daniel got louder and cried harder. With him at my feet throwing a stunning tantrum and the girls making a mess of my closet in the bedroom, I couldn't apply my makeup without shaking. It was so sad. Anyone looking in from the outside would feel bad for me, and that's exactly how I felt; I felt bad for me.

So there I sat on the bathroom floor weeping like the toddler before me. I couldn't help it. My body could not think to do anything else. I just wanted to get dressed. That's all. I wanted to get dressed and be on time for a dinner date with my husband. Instead, I was being harassed by a two-year-old boy and distracted by little girls yelping in delight as they gained momentum in their enthusiasm to unload another closet. This sort of stimulation paralyzed me. I sat on the floor of the bathroom listening to the chaos of my life, and cried. Eventually I got to my feet and looked around. It was surreal. My house was in shambles. The girls had pulled everything out of the closets, the closets in every room. And Daniel, well, he was still in top form, his lungs not yet exhausted.

At this point, my body went into some sort of "fight or flight" response, although I think it was more like "fight *and* flight." I didn't physically leave the house, but I metaphorically left my body for a few minutes. I began to ramble, while weeping (ranting and raving) about how hard it was to be a mother in this house. I kept saying, "I don't want to do this anymore—it's too hard." I know now that I was saying things that I should never have said in the presence of my children. But as I said, I had left my body, and I was fighting for my survival at the same time. Those were fighting words, no doubt. In any case, you need to hear what happened next.

Despite my frantic state of mind, I could hear my girls fighting downstairs. They did something I had never heard them do before. They were threatening to hurt each other physically. Leigh Ann was daring Laura to hit her, and Laura was yelling that she was going to punch Leigh Ann in the face. I can laugh about this now, but it certainly wasn't funny then. It was tragic, and I realized that even as I stood upstairs listening. Unfortunately, though, I was too paralyzed and upset by the chaos to intervene, and so I just listened and hoped that no one would get hurt too badly. At that moment my brother Bill arrived, ready to babysit for the evening. He may have been startled by the commotion but had the wherewithal to separate the girls and take Daniel from me. I was obviously frazzled. In an effort to console me, he said something that has stayed with me until this day. He said, "You are just having a bad moment. You have lots of moments with the kids and many of them good moments. This one is a bad moment, that's all." I knew he was right, but I could not embrace that logic through the tension in the air. I continued to get dressed and left the house as fast as I could. Later that evening, while talking to my husband, I shared what had happened and how I thought I was starting to have too many bad moments, the effect of which was becoming apparent in the children. I was stressed out, and the children were showing it.

The point of this story is to illustrate tone. Tone is similar to ambience; it is an atmospheric quality set in motion by a particular environment. Within a household, tone is set by a variety of factors and personalities; however, a mother generally sets the tone in a home more than anyone (or anything) else. She sets the tone in various ways, such as the décor, rules, and expectations she applies. However, her mood and behavior impact tone to the greatest degree; they directly affect the mood and behavior of every other member of the family, especially the children. Children tend to *absorb* the mood and energy of their mothers. Children "know" Mom's mood from their first interaction with her. They can't articulate it, analyze it, or rationalize it, but they certainly absorb it throughout the day. Have you ever noticed how children seem to act worse when their parents feel desperate for them to cooperate? That's because children sense the tension, the desperation, and then act in ways that release the stress that they have internalized. Acting out is how children typically express the negative feelings they sense.

When a mother feels stressed out, a child will likely feed off the stress and become stress-full (i.e., full of stress). He or she will evidence this stress in a multitude of ways; however, it is often displayed in negative or annoying ways. In very young children, it often shows itself in whining and in the desperate plea, via crying or temper tantrum, to be held by no one other than Mom. In older children it might take the form of a bad habit, such as nail biting or hair twisting (common childhood habits). It could also show up in bad attitudes, obnoxious behavior, bedwetting, and aggressive behaviors such as biting or hitting other children.

Debbie, a mother of two, shares this story:

It happened about a year ago. I was getting ready for a family outing. Although I was excited, I felt stressed to keep on schedule with the other members of my family, particularly my sister, who planned on leaving especially early. I remember racing through the house collecting toys for the car in one hand and juggling my five-month-old in the other hand. The clock was ticking, the baby needed changing, the car had to be packed, and my three-year-old son was demanding attention, begging to be picked up. He wanted juice, his truck, anything that would take me away from what I was trying to accomplish. And I had lots to accomplish. Like most moms, I had a mental checklist of things I wanted to bring and things I had to do before we left the house. [Checklists always take so long to complete, and this one was no exception.]

Debbie continues with the details:

I knew the tension was mounting, but I was still eager to keep on schedule. I put the baby down in the house and walked out to the car, closing the door behind me so that I could take a quiet moment to look at the car and pack what was necessary. I just wanted to get it done and get going. I left my son inside crying for me, but I wanted to go alone. Well, my son must have been writhing with frustration inside the house. He was alone with the baby and had never ever hurt the baby before so it never occurred to me that he might. But he did. He was hitting her or at least that is what it sounded like from her screaming. I ran into the house and stopped him before he seriously hurt her. He was completely out of control, as was I.

They were all out of control. Anger, fear, helplessness, and frustration had reached an unbearable height and it was being expressed uniquely by each of them. Within minutes, and still full of rage, Debbie grabbed her son and literally tossed him onto his bed. She confessed to hitting him while screaming, "Don't you ever hit the baby, not ever!" Debbie's fury not only blinded the irony of her actions (hitting her son while telling him "don't hit"), but it brought on the guilt that usually follows an incident like this. What's especially ironic is that Debbie felt more stressed out after hitting her son than she did before this incident, and her son was more desperate than ever for his mother's attention.

Through similar stories, enough mothers have supported my argument that a mother's mood invariably affects her children's mood, and ultimately their behavior. Children are remarkable in their ability to sense their mother's mood and internalize it. No matter what emotion a mother is feeling, a child can sense it and then reflect it back in subtle or demonstrative ways (e.g., biting, hitting, crying). As an experiment, notice your children's behavior when you're feeling anxious, depressed, angry, melancholy, or unresponsive. Notice the mood in the house, whether it's tense or loud, quiet or chaotic. Now make the conscious decision to put aside your stress and your negative mood. As hard as it is, change. Tell the kids that you don't want to be in a bad mood and then suggest going out to get an ice cream. Or walk into the room where the children are and play music. Take your child's hand and begin to dance with him or her. Chase your children and tickle them. Suggest they help you make dinner and have fun doing it. Involve them. In other words, make your children smile in any way that works. And then look again at your children's behavior. Notice the way they treat each other and you. Observe the changes in mood that occur in the house, the feeling in the air that I refer to as tone.

I have spent much time experimenting with tone and my ability to affect it, both at home and away from home. Often I have been in situations outside the home when I wanted or needed my children to be well behaved and cooperative, whether we were at someone else's house or a public event. Either scenario creates its share of stress for a parent because the pressure is on and others are watching. During these outings, I tend to be anxious right from the start. However, it's usually in one gesture or action that I reveal this anxiety. Perhaps it's in the subtle change in my breathing pattern or the tension in my hand as I wrap my fingers around someone's arm. Regardless of what it is, I know when my mood has been detected because my children begin to test my resolve. They push to see how loud I will get, how angry I will become in public. All the while, I'm smiling as my grip tightens. This little dance goes on for quite some time as the tone among us becomes more ugly and obvious. Since I am aware of tone, I understand that I could leave the situation as quickly as possible and sidestep tone altogether or I could stay and let go of the anxiety that's feeding my children.

To dispel anxiety, I have shared my feelings with the people around me in the hope that they will allay my concerns and forgive the chaos that might descend upon them at any moment. Or I have simply embraced the potential for embarrassment, shaking my head the whole time as if to say, "Whatever." When I *truly* let go of my anxiety, I've noticed that my children behave in ways that are not at all disruptive to anyone; in fact, they become more cooperative, or maybe just less conspicuous. I am more relaxed and engage them in better spirits (nicer voice, gentler touch, etc.), which makes them far more responsive to my requests. In other words, my children move further away from the behaviors I fear, thus removing my cause for anxiety. In effect, we create a new dance. Overall, I can affect tone out in public, but I do think it's harder for me because I feel the social pressure (whether perceived or actual) to "control" my children, a pressure that can sabotage my presence of mind and my ability to redirect a wayward tone. As a result, I have left social events rather abruptly on occasion, swearing never to go out with my kids again, until, of course, we go out again.

At home things are different. I don't have to worry about what anyone thinks about my children or their behavior. I am usually home alone to endure the tone for better or worse, so it's certainly in my best interest to understand the dynamics of setting tone. With three young children, the tone in my house can change often and without notice. My son can become frustrated with his inability to express his needs adequately and become ornery in an instant. Or my daughters can start fighting because there is only one pair of princess slippers and four feet wanting them. As for me, even if the day starts out nicely, I might grow weary and plagued by burnout long before it's anyone's bedtime, which means that I can become ornery myself much too easily. Having said all this, one can see that all day, every day, the tone is up for grabs, and the tone can change throughout the day. We all contribute to the tone on an hourly basis, but I know from experience that my children take their cues from me.

When I'm physically spent and feeling emotionally "broken," I don't have the capacity to care for my children in a way that I think is expected of me. When I'm feeling sad, angry, depressed, or anxious, I feel stuck. I feel trapped in my own world, isolated and unable to conjure up the energy, focus, and desire to help my children in whatever way they need me. I've also noticed that I begin to resent the care they need, which looks and feels like I resent them. This brings about a whole slew of other feelings. From there, it is pretty much downhill in terms of how I feel, the tone I present, and, of course, how my children respond to my mood and the tone that I've created. My girls tend to develop a frenzied-like energy, which leads to more chaos and fighting. And my son cries more. Their behavior reminds me of the adage "Negative attention is better than no attention at all" because they certainly get my attention and my response is nothing short of negative. I usually explode, crying or screaming about the house, which of course solidifies the bad tone.

On the other hand, when I feel "whole," strong, and happy I make light of almost everything that happens in the house. I have the patience to teach my son how to better articulate his needs or at least lighten his mood by distracting him with a fun activity. I also have the mental acuity to help my girls figure out ways that they can negotiate a win-win solution for all the things they fight over. I have access to my sense of humor and have fun with my children. Problems don't seem as big and the messes are less annoying. My children aren't afraid of me and they choose to act in ways they know will please me. We come together in a synergy of energy that makes the house a nice place to be; a house where the children are happy and enjoy being with each other and with me. Of course the tone in the house can still change quickly and adversely, but I have the capacity to redirect the tone just as quickly because I feel grounded; I am neither weak nor disabled by the strain of feeling lost or broken. I embrace the fact that among all the members of my family, I have the greatest capability to affect tone; however, my capacity to affect a desired tone *relies on my ability to choose* a more desirable tone and change my own mood and behavior to reflect that decision.

Power of Choice

How readily a mother can stop a bad mood and turn a smile depends on many things, such as innate personality, circumstances (e.g., finances, marital status), parenting skills, familial or communal support, and overall health. These factors usually combine in some way to distinguish how a mother handles the inherent challenges that her children pose on a daily basis. Above and beyond these factors, though, is a critical component in determining whether a mother can alter her mood when adversely affected by these challenges. That component is the power of choice. A mother must choose to change her mood and behavior in order to effect the change she desires in herself and in her children. After many interviews and lots of soul searching, I believe that a mother's capacity to make this choice relies heavily, almost exclusively, on her mental and emotional stability and well-being. This is not to confuse well-being with perpetual happiness. By emotional well-being I mean that a mother can tolerate a certain degree of psychological distress without it compromising her perceptions; that is, how she perceives her sense of self and how she perceives her children.

I interviewed Margot, who maintained a healthy perception of self despite some tough days she had with her young children. Margot admitted that it was far harder to be with her children than she assumed it would be when she decided to quit her job and stay home as a full-time mom. However, she continued to feel positive about her decision, her ability to care for her children, and her vision of self despite the stress and strain she felt as she adjusted to her new role.

Margot

I consider myself a smart and strong woman. I'm the kind of person who knows what has to be done, and I do it. Staying home with my kids certainly pushes me to be more patient, loving, and present than I've ever had to be, but I'm doing it. At first, it was kind of strange to be home all day, with the kids, all day, with them, all day [laughing] but as the days passed, I grew into the part and sort of paced myself. I had to come up with things to do, places to go, people to see, but it's part of my job. It's what I do now. And it's okay. I love seeing the kids more. I mean, don't get me wrong. I can have some pretty bad days when I feel tired, frustrated, or bored with what I'm doing. Sometimes I have to lock Claire in her car seat for a break [laughing], but I can usually figure out how to get what I need when I need it. And then I can take care of Claire and Matt again. I mean, with two kids, you have to remember to make Mommy happy first.

In contrast, I interviewed Donna, who felt as though she was "dying." Quick to emphasize her love for her children, Donna seemed self-conscious and awkward as she admitted to "feelings that I have never shared with anyone." She cried throughout the interview and actually hung her head as she voiced some self-reflections.

Donna

I yell at my kids all the time. I don't know what's wrong with me. [Pause] I used to be nice to be with. I don't like what I've become. [Pause] I don't like how I look, how I act, how I feel, or anything else about my life right now. I'm just miserable. I can hardly stand talking to you about all this. It's embarrassing. You must think I'm a horrible mom.

I assured Donna that her feelings were not unusual. In fact, I had used the word "dying" myself on more than one occasion several years ago. It sounds extreme, but the word is often used as a metaphor to convey the desperate need for sustenance, the things in life one wants or needs in order to feel alive. So I continued on, asking Donna more questions about her life, herself, and her family. In our short time together, it was obvious that Donna's psychological distress had reached a point where her perceptions were distorted. This was easy to discern because she was consistently using expressions such as "all the time," "never," and "always." Few things in life occur "all the time," "never," or "always." Her discourse was extreme, unlikely to be true in reality, and reflective of a person in crisis. I explored with Donna what may have been missing from her life that led her to feel so discontent and depressed. In that conversation, I heard mostly about her marriage. She rarely saw her husband because he worked two jobs to support the family. Donna also missed her friends from work. Later she elaborated on her physical appearance, in particular, how she had gained weight since staying home. All in all, I heard about losses, one after another. Her crisis of loss had ultimately affected her overall sense of self, and she felt as though she was dying.

When in the crisis of loss, mothers are far less able to exercise their power of choice. To make a choice requires thought, and to act on those choices requires effort. This kind of thought and effort doesn't come easily when a mother is handicapped by the physical, cognitive, social, or emotional symptoms associated with the crisis of loss (i.e., grief) that I've described in this book. Imagine times of loss in general. Imagine how hard it would be for anyone to care for a child when grieving the loss of a significant other, a needed job, or a very special memento. I would assume that the myriad reactions to the loss would render a person incapable of caring for a child (or one's self) as well as he or she might care for a child (or one's self) under different circumstances. I would further assume that the grieving individual would struggle just to get through the day, and understandably so. "Struggling to get through the day" is a common expression among the mothers I interviewed. When a mother struggles to get through her day, she is certainly not up to the challenge of altering her emotional state to create a pleasant atmosphere. From personal experience, I can attest to the fact that when I'm struggling to get through a day, my goal for the day is not to create a positive tone in the house but rather to provide the basic care my children need until I put them to bed.

To embrace the concept of choice and the power to create a positive tone, a mother must be free from the various symptoms that would otherwise afflict her when grieving. In my work as a grief counselor, I discovered that symptoms, especially emotional symptoms, slowly dissipate as grieving individuals understand the meaning of loss in their lives and accept the path that their grief has taken. Therefore, I believe that mothers experiencing MIA are likely to understand and accept how they think, act, and feel once they recognize how their perception of change reveals loss, how loss infiltrates their experience of motherhood, and how their sense of self may have been threatened. With this understanding, mothers may be capable of pursuing the grief work that's necessary to move past grief and toward the process of reclaiming their sense of self so that they may create the changes they desire, whether in themselves, in their children, or in their homes. The ability to direct a tone among family members is an empowering experience. The capacity to set a desirable tone is an enormous opportunity that can change lives, particularly the lives of the mothers who exercise their power of choice to do so. The choices that mothers make do yield the results they achieve. However, mothers must be *able* to access their power of choice, which depends on a healthy sense of self and the emotional well-being that supports that health.

SIX:
THE BOUNDARY HUNTER

o o o o o o o o o o o o o o o o o o o o o o o o o o o o o o

"To live through an impossible situation, you don't need the reflexes of a Grand Prix driver, the muscles of a Hercules, the mind of an Einstein. You simply need to know what to do."

—*Anthony Greenbank,* **The Book of Survival**

Just the other day while food shopping, I saw a mother standing approximately four feet from her shopping cart. Her toddler son was climbing vigorously about the car that was attached to the cart. She was standing still with her hands covering her mouth, looking haggard and miserable. Not sure if I should intervene, I timidly asked if she was all right. She looked at me with glassy eyes and said, "I feel like throwing up." Within seconds she continued, "He's in rare form today." In an instant, I realized she was not physically ill, just wound up beyond her comfort level. She spoke again, "He's wearing me down. I really feel like I can throw up." She may as well have said that he was wearing her away because that is exactly how she looked to me, like a shell of a woman. My heart went out to her, having been there myself many times. I offered to help, but she assured me that she would be fine. I continued on my way, knowing she had lied to me in an uncomfortable and self-conscious moment. Throughout the day, I thought about this woman. I figured this incident was not the first or only stressful occasion in her life as a mother, and I knew that it wouldn't be her last.

As I've mentioned throughout this book, motherhood demands that women produce, provide, and satisfy on a daily basis. They must discipline, sacrifice, and tolerate a tremendous amount every day. This call to action can stress a woman's sense of self. However, in the pages that follow, I suggest ways for mothers to reclaim and/or secure their sense of self. In reclaiming and maintaining a sense of self, mothers are better able to live their lives from a position of strength and engage others in ways that promote long-term mental, emotional, physical, social, spiritual, sexual, and intellectual good health. These suggestions along with grief work (Chapter 7) are the things that helped me find solace, strength, *and* the familiar aspects of myself that had long since vanished in the chaos of my life. Before all other suggestions, though, I urge mothers to establish and embrace some basic "rights." As an example, I have listed some rights that stand strong in my life today, rights that I declare out loud from time to time, especially in moments that test me. In no particular order of significance:

> I have a right to my feelings.
> I have a right to talk about these feelings.
> I have a right to expect understanding and support.
> I have a right to physical and mental/emotional limits.
> I have a right to fully develop into the person I desire to become.
> I have a right to pursue my goals, hobbies, and ambitions.
> I have a right to experience a bad moment, or two.
> I have a right to say, "NO."
> I have a right to say, "Go Away" or "Leave me alone."
> I have a right to ask for help, and get it.
> I have a right to search for meaning.
> I have a right to be angry, depressed, anxious, irritable, or whatever I may feel when in the company of my children when they are sabotaging my well-being.
> I have a right to be happy and fulfilled.
> I have a right to have my needs satisfied.
> I have a right to dream and have the space/time/quiet necessary to think about those dreams in a way that will advance me toward the fulfillment of those dreams.
> I have a right to mourn the things that I miss.

Remember, these are my rights and I may write them however I wish. It's empowering to write them down, see them, and say them out loud. Greater still is the act of enforcing them. Imagine how good it would feel to write down and enforce your own set of rights. The following mothers took on this exercise and expressed rights I thought were very compelling.

Liz

I have a right to end conversations with people who make me feel bad about myself or my parenting.
I have a right not to be responsible for every behavior my children exhibit.
I have a right to experience life on my terms.

Judy

I have a right to be "good enough."
I have a right to relax and be frivolous.

Brenda

I have a right to evolve in my role as a mother, wife, and woman.
I have a right to make decisions that seem selfish.
I have a right to make a phone call in quiet and pee with the door closed.

Lisa M.

I have a right to say "no" to anything that violates my boundaries or my dignity.
I have a right to respect simply because I am me.
I have a right to feel unsure, frightened, and confused.

Angie

I have a right to my memories and the way I remember them.
I have a right to forgive myself for all that I am not.

Susan

I have a right to make new friends and keep the ones I already have.

Tara

I have a right to sleep through the night or feel cranky if I don't.
I have a right to take my time.

I have a right to sit while I eat.
I have a right to ask my husband to serve dinner or at least clean up after we eat.
I have a right to be honest about my feelings when asked about being a full-time stay-at-home mom.

Melanie

I have a right to exercise my power of choice.
I have a right to make mistakes.
I have a right to keep adding to my list of rights.

In an effort to reclaim your sense of self, I suggest you compose *your* list of rights. Take your time and think through how to protect your sanity and your sense of self. Don't worry about the words you use or how others might interpret them. Allow for at least five rights. Anything short of five rights implies that you are not as important as the other members of your family, which is absurd. Of course it may be difficult to formulate your rights if you don't know what you want, need, desire, and prefer. I was amazed to learn the number of mothers who seldom even think about themselves in this context; the mothers I interviewed took minutes to answer the questions I asked, and in fact couldn't answer some of them at all. Listed below are questions I designed to fuel the search for self. Try to think outside the box you call home; that is, answer the questions so that they reflect you and not the role you play as mother. I intentionally asked similar questions to weed out what may have been forgotten over time. Write your answer in the space provided after each question.

What do you like most about yourself?

How would you most like to feel?

Who makes you feel good about yourself and why?

How often do you see this person?

What personal affront makes you most angry?

What do you admire most about yourself?

What do you feel most passionate about?

When you daydream, what do you see?

What's one thing you really want to do?

What are you most enthusiastic about?

What's one thing you'd like to see happen?

What do you enjoy doing most by yourself?

What's one talent you possess?

What do you want to do most of all?

What's your favorite way to procrastinate?

What skill or talent would you love to possess?

What does your "child within" ask of you?

What's one good thought that can distract you?

What's one impulse you'd like to act on?

What's one way you'd like to see yourself grow?

What do you do when you are all alone?

What would you do if you had more time?

What would you do if you had more money?

What do you wish you could create?

What does your ideal day look like?

What does your ideal self look like?

When you were young, what did you want to become?

If you were to give yourself one present, what would it be?

What activity causes you to forget time and the rest of the world?

What do you yearn for?

What is your greatest strength?

What makes you most angry or resentful?

When do you feel most content?

What do you love to do so much that you would be willing to pay money to do it?

Look for a pattern in the answers you provided. Your answers will reveal the thoughts, beliefs, feelings, needs, desires, hopes, and experiences that are not usually declared out loud. Your answers also express what you value. For example, you may describe things that suggest your need or desire for achievement, power, wealth, wisdom, inner harmony, affection, adventure, friendship, humor, creativity, loyalty, self-respect, freedom, fame, economic security, spirituality, family, health, order, or personal development. In fact, this is only a sample of the values I ascertained from the women I interviewed; it is not an all-inclusive list. Recently, I perceived "recognition" as a value one mother esteemed. Although she had voluntarily (and happily) resigned from a prestigious company to stay home with her children, she did express a desire for acknowledgment, a desire for the status and satisfaction often associated with something such as a promotion (which eludes motherhood, no doubt!).

As it implies, a value is something we recognize as important and meaningful. Collectively, our values structure our true self. *Knowing* what we value is helpful, but *owning* those values is essential, especially as mothers seek to recover the sense of self that vanished. In owning what is important and meaningful, mothers strengthen their sense of self, which in turn reinforces their values. Taking ownership of our significant values is most often marked by the decisions we make and the actions we take; that is, *ownership of our values is obvious in the boundaries we create.* A boundary declares to others where a line must be drawn to preserve our comfort level. A physical boundary may be as obvious as a fence, whereas a social boundary as subtle as a step back from those who stand too close. Likewise we can establish boundaries to declare at what point we feel manipulated, taken advantage of, or extended beyond reason. Boundaries act as a set of limits that preserve our personal identity, uniqueness, and autonomy; they safeguard those aspects of our lives that create an optimal degree of emotional, physical, psychological, mental, social, and spiritual well-being. In other words, boundaries protect our values and the aspects of our selves that evidence in those values.

Creating Boundaries
Step One

The first step in creating a boundary is to acknowledge the beliefs, thoughts, dreams, feelings, preferences, needs, experiences, activities, etc., that occupy your inner life, your private thoughts—the answers you established in the previous exercise. If you could not successfully answer the questions posed in that exercise and feel that you don't have enough insight into your values, you might consider meditation or prayer, keeping a journal, or talking to a trusted friend. Some women find mental health professionals especially effective in helping them access answers because therapists often employ experiential and structured techniques, such as hypnosis, psychodrama, storytelling, dream analysis, guided imagery, or other modalities that encourage feedback and insight into a client's inner (unconscious and subconscious) life.

Another way mothers may obtain insight into their values is by paying attention to those moments that spark intense (and usually negative) reactions, otherwise known in the world of psychotherapy as *abreactions*. You can think of an abreaction as an overreaction. An overreaction generally signals the anger, tension, and frustration one feels when one's needs/wants are not being met. For instance, I become ornery and very ugly right around 9 p.m. if my children are still awake. It's at that hour when I desperately desire to become Anne again, and do the things that Anne likes to do ALONE. Anyone standing in the way of that desire sees my wrath. So take notice, take notes, and be honest. There's an unfulfilled need or want that inspires your abreaction; maybe even a dream that was dashed or a goal that was subdued. Ask yourself, "What did I want that I didn't get?" You may have to dig deep or wait patiently, but the answer should emerge and provide a value. In my example, I wanted to be alone, which reflects my values of inner harmony, peace, and individuality.

In contrast, I have also realized some of my key values when a need or want was *fulfilled*. For instance, snuggling in bed with my husband on a wintry night satisfies my need for love, security, peace, and intimacy. Playing with my children grips my desire for fun, joy, and synergy. Writing promotes my sense of autonomy, creativity, and mastery. And dinner out with Danya integrates my values of friendship, humor, and understanding. Knowing what I value allows me to recognize when a value is being denied. So look twice at those moments when you lose your temper or when you retreat into martyrdom. Pay attention when you become aloof, detached, or even over-enmeshed. Identify your reactions to certain situations and become familiar with the ways in which you respond to having your boundaries violated so that you know exactly when it's happening. Once you have identified the ways in which you respond to having your boundaries violated (and the stimulus for that response), determine the irrational thinking that is typically associated with such reactions. Listen to what you are saying to yourself when you have a strong reaction (internally or externally) at a time when a need or want is being neglected, denied or ignored. You may be rationalizing the behaviors of others, rationalizing your own behavior, or worse still, shaming yourself.

Step Two

Once you determine your most significant values, you must set the boundaries that will protect those values; boundaries that will safeguard your sense of self against the people, roles, and responsibilities that are intentionally/unintentionally, innocently, or indirectly sabotaging your efforts to stay intact as a mentally sound, content, healthy, and prospering woman. Boundaries are most effective when they are flexible enough to bend when necessary, but strong enough to snap back when required. A good boundary knows when to say "no," but acquiesces when the limits are understood. For instance, I'm a rational person with healthy boundaries, so when my daughter has a good reason to be awake after 9 p.m., I don't become irate or unempathic. Rather, I work toward resolving the issue at hand with the understanding that my needs may have been sacrificed this time, but salvaged in the morning when I rearrange my commitments to allow for what I lost the night before. A limit was set, my needs were met, and I moved forward before another night was upon me. I did not forsake my needs; I indulged them shortly after the "sabotage." By doing this, I don't become resentful, burned out, or symptomatic of a woman lost in the unpredictable, demanding, and all-consuming role of mother.

We set boundaries by being honest, identifying needs, wants, goals, etc., and setting limits. Creating boundaries requires patience, clarity, consistency, and a firm but gentle voice. In a nutshell, setting a boundary requires that you accomplish three tasks.

1. Adjust any irrational thinking that is attached to former ways of acting or speaking that allowed boundaries to be violated.

2. Express both verbally and nonverbally what is acceptable and what is not. State what you *specifically* need, want, and prefer by describing the when, how often, what kind, and with whom of your needs, wants, and preferences. In being clear and forthright, you express the limits to which you can comfortably go before the sense of self you value starts to fade.

3. Act in ways that support what you establish verbally. Act in ways that support healthy boundaries, ways that endorse living without the need for approval, and ways that are free of the fear associated with rejection. Act by being assertive and setting goals, and above all, act by saying "no" to things you don't want to do.

For example, I remember times when I was eager to leave the house by myself so I could do something that was important to me. I also remember becoming frustrated on many occasions because I was continually being summoned by a family member to do one final task before leaving. As I stomped angrily around the house I would think, "I'll do it. Who else is going to do it? This is the last thing and then I'm leaving." It was rarely the last thing, and I always felt short-changed as the clock ticked away my free time. The anger was the signal, and my irrational thinking had me believing that I was the only person responsible for the needs of the family. I learned how to say, "I'm out of here." And lo and behold, they took care of themselves and figured out how to get what they wanted without me. I *acted* in accordance with a *newer, more rational perspective*, which I declared *verbally* in a precise and defined way.

In setting healthy and appropriate boundaries, mothers discourage children, spouses, family, and friends from repeatedly exploiting the fundamental values that exist at their core. Likewise, they exercise the set of rights central to their unique identity and lifestyle. Healthy boundaries serve to protect the integrity of the self and what the self needs to thrive. Boundaries are not intended to hurt, control, or manipulate others (this would be narcissistic). Boundaries simply stand between a mother's overall well-being and the things and people that jeopardize that well-being.

SEVEN:
GRIEF IN ACTION

o o o o o o o o o o o o o o o o o o o o o o o o o o o o o o o o o
"I do not believe that sheer suffering teaches. If suffering alone taught, all the world would be wise since everyone suffers. To suffering must be added mourning, understanding, patience, love, openness and the willingness to remain vulnerable."

—Anne Morrow Lindbergh

When a significant other transforms reality through his or her *death,* a "survivor" must adjust from a life that *was* to a life that *is.* When a baby transforms reality through his or her *birth,* women must adjust from a life that was to a life that is. On opposite ends of the spectrum, each experience yields a transforming moment, a moment that provides avenues for learning, growth, and, for some, a sense of peace. Realizing this, I wanted to take my opportunity, my transforming moment, and become more. Staying stagnant, in distress, was no longer an option. I was in a new world and it called me to move. However, as I mentioned in Chapter 5, in order to move, that is, in order to access my power of choice to act, I had to have a healthy sense of self, which I didn't perceive myself as having at the time. So how could I choose a better way of coping? How could I choose to move into a better place emotionally, physically, socially, etc.? How could I choose to change my experience of the life circumstances around me? How could I choose health and happiness over my existing distress? I needed to make choices and take action, and yet I didn't have the healthy sense of self that spearheads those choices and actions.

This paradox plagued me until one night when the answer came to me as I lay in bed crying. In that glorious and enlightened moment, I realized this: The actual act of grieving is an action in and of itself. The word "grieving" suggests that something is happening, and behind every "happening" is an action taking place. To promote grieving as the full range of our coping responses is to offer mothers a useful paradigm that can empower them to act, as it may for all those who experience loss and grief. It's a concept that defies the powerlessness and helplessness that mothers often feel as their sense of self wanes. A feeling of helplessness/powerlessness or lack of choice (feeling trapped) causes much of the symptoms mothers describe, especially depression, anxiety, despair, and the inability to act on their own behalf (i.e., paralysis). Grieving as coping reframes the process and puts the locus of control in the hands of those mothers who battle these intense symptoms. Grieving as coping inspires mothers to respond actively and invest the energy necessary for redirecting their lives; they do this by accepting the fact that they have a voice and can make the choices that support their values, boundaries, and sense of self. In this way, they break loose of helplessness, resist the potent and sometimes compelling grip of grief, and create a new posture geared toward making the changes they desire through the choices they make. The critical choices available to mothers include but are not limited to:

- how they deal with the various challenges that present on a daily basis
- how they respond to the losses they perceive
- how to reshape, reinterpret, and redirect their lives
- how to find their sense of self
- how to sort their needs, options, and preferences
- how to define the next chapter of their lives
- how to change their internal dialogue, and last but by no means least,
- how to start making these choices

I have found over the years that oftentimes we are told what to do but not precisely *how* to do it. At least that was my dilemma as I struggled to find my way out of the crater of despair that had become my nesting spot. At the time, I read article after article looking for material that might suggest ways to help me adjust to a reality far different from anything I had ever known. I perused books on motherhood, childcare, and mental health (I thought I was going crazy), all in an attempt to "figure it out." I couldn't find one book, not one article, not one television show that comforted me with information that directly addressed all the feelings and thoughts I was having.

As I saw it, my "problem" was that I did not adopt a total posture of "mom" as soon as my baby was born. I mothered my daughter and cared for her in all the ways she needed as my love deepened, but in many ways, I remained postured as I had been prior to Leigh Ann's arrival. Subconsciously, I perceived myself to be the same person who was able to live the same kind of life in the same way. In short, I *desired* the impossible (e.g., former freedoms, relationships, autonomy, lifestyle) *knowing* full well it was an impossible reality given my new circumstances. It was a dissonance that lay dormant for years. In the meantime, I gave birth to Laura (sixteen months later) and Daniel, who came along three years after her. By this time I was deeply entrenched in the world of children and becoming more and more incapable of denying or ignoring my desire for the autonomy, self-confidence, self-esteem, and sense of self I once knew. I felt completely out of sync with a life rhythm I had always known and enjoyed, and this feeling was making me increasingly angry, depressed, and frustrated.

I lingered in grief for several years. Ironically, I wanted control in my life that allowed for the changes I wanted and the conditions I sought, yet I remained in the state of grief, which fostered my feelings of helplessness, anger, depression, and anxiety. As a therapist, I understood that emotions generally motivate people to take action; it just took me a long time to integrate the concept. Once I did, I used grief to motivate me to act. I became motivated to make the choices that were available to me so that I could develop a new life rhythm, so to speak. I aspired toward a rhythm that incorporated aspects of my former self that I valued while considering the fact that I was the mother of three adorably delightful but needy children. With the significance of harmony ever so present, I focused on what *was* possible and how I could make that happen; in other words, *I recognized and embraced the fact that I was not choiceless; I was capable of making many choices that would affect me and my life in a positive way.*

I started this process by accepting help. I suppose that was my first choice. I could hide in the attic and cry time and time again or I could agree to the help my husband offered when he found me sitting in the attic crying. The conversation went something like this within a few minutes:

My husband:
"Why don't you find someone to help you around here? Do you need me to take over and find someone or figure out what to do?"

Me:
"Yes, I do. I don't know what's wrong with me. I can't seem to figure it out. I'm so unhappy. I don't know why I don't get someone to help me. I'm just stuck in this bad place where I can't seem to help myself."

My husband:
"All right, I'll make some calls and see what I can find out. I've got so much going on at work, so I'll find someone to help you around the house during the day. What else can I do?"

Me:
"I don't know."

This simple gesture, this one simple conversation turned my life around. Within days my husband introduced me to Irena, a fabulous young lady from the Czech Republic. Although I was very apprehensive about having a "stranger" in my house with my children, I slowly let go of that anxiety as my spirits and energy picked up. With time and energy newly available, I was able to think about *me*. I thought about my life, what I wanted for myself, and how to achieve the things I considered most important. Focusing on *my* development was refreshing and insightful. One of the many things I realized was that *I couldn't problem solve while in the crisis; I was too overwhelmed to see the options available to me*. I also realized that my symptoms, conflicting feelings, and negative internal dialogue were dissipating as I directed energy toward *my* needs and wants. In satisfying key needs and wants, I was becoming more familiar to myself and less incapacitated by the symptoms that had only recently disabled me. A search and rescue effort was set in motion the day I met Irena and acquiesced to the help that was being offered. Irena worked for us for one year, which was enough time for me to reclaim my sense of self, take stock of my life, and complete a large portion of this book. A year may not be necessary for other mothers who want to consider a "nanny," as personal needs and circumstances vary. However, as I have learned, *scheduled* help is invaluable when a crisis is at hand.

So it happened for me that my husband and Irena intervened. In conversation with other mothers, I learned of other ways that women find relief. For instance, some women consented to medication, which served its purpose and eased symptoms sufficiently to allow lost coping skills to resurrect. I also heard about supermarkets and gyms with babysitting services that gave respite to mothers who wanted to eat quietly or spin away (literally and figuratively) for a couple of hours a day. If you are feeling miserable and unable to move yourself toward the people and places that can offer you a break, you are seriously overwhelmed. In this case, you need to stop and recall how you coped in the past when times were tough. Recall an occasion or event in your past when you felt ill prepared, extremely frustrated, or helpless. Think about what you did or who helped you. Recalling an effective coping skill might be what it takes to revive it and move you far enough to reach the critical phase of reclaiming your sense of self, a phase focused on goals.

The ten goals outlined below are intended to facilitate a woman's movement away from the grief she may be experiencing and toward the equilibrium found in health and healing. They are goals aligned with how to make an easier transition into motherhood and how to process the multitude of feelings and thoughts that tend to emerge for women as they devote themselves entirely to each and every child placed ever so delicately in their arms. The goals focus on the issues most central in the feelings of loss many women experience as they become over-wrought in their efforts to mother well.

GOALS

1. Identify your values (review Chapter 6)

2. Create boundaries to secure your values (review Chapter 6)

3. Acknowledge losses associated with motherhood

4. Express emotions related to your experience of motherhood and feel-ings of loss

5. Modify relationships into what's realistic

6. Identify and recover what is still viable from your former self and lifestyle

7. Regain capacities impaired by stress

8. Recognize the dissonance that exists between life before and after children

9. Relearn the world (see next chapter)

10. Relearn your self; reestablish your sense of self (see next chapter)

Acknowledge Losses Associated with Motherhood

Mothers need to think through their lives and see the changes that took place as they transitioned into motherhood. Once they recognize the changes, they can better assess whether or not those changes elicit feelings of loss. If feelings of loss register, *it's important to consider and name each loss individually.* I called it My Miss List. My Miss List included a pair of jeans that fit me perfectly at size 6; moments of solitude and moments alone with my husband; good friends whom I neglected to keep "in the loop" as days turned into months and years; and eating food while it was hot. Chapter 2, "What's There to Lose?" identifies six kinds of loss and examples of each. They include material loss, relationship loss, functional loss, intrapsychic loss, role loss, and systemic loss. Review Chapter 2 as needed.

Express Your Emotions

During interviews, a surprisingly large number of mothers admitted that they never shared their feelings with their husbands, friends, or family of origin (i.e., mother, father, siblings). It seems that fear prevents many women from sharing—fear associated with rejection, embarrassment, ridicule, judgment, and shame. Fear prevents mothers from reaching out and getting the support, encouragement, help, and advice they seek and deserve. If fear exists, I suggest mothers commiserate with other mothers at a support group, since these mothers will most likely appreciate all the emotions attached to motherhood and not judge even the "worst" of feelings. *A support group is a great place to practice expressing the difficult feelings and thoughts that may be important for family members to eventually hear.* In addition, a review of Chapter 3, "About Grief," will help mothers recognize the various feelings, thoughts, and symptoms often associated with grief, in the event they are uncertain as to what they are expressing and why.

Modify Relationships into What's Realistic

Relationships are constantly evolving as will your transition into motherhood. As mothers, we will constantly be adjusting and adapting to the new life circumstances, problems, and pleasures that each developmental stage offers our children. Likewise, our marriages adjust and adapt to the stresses, strains, and awakenings that naturally occur over the course of time. Having said this, it's reasonable to expect that with the advent of motherhood, many if not all relationships will undergo transformation, particularly between husband and wife. Every marriage I know rattled at least a little when a baby came along. Some husbands became jealous of the baby, others lonely for their partner and friend. Wise couples anticipate this and plan "dates" to keep their relationship kindled. However, all the dates in the world can't change the fact that Mom is now somewhat, if not totally, preoccupied with baby, and Dad feels it. Again, it's normal and will likely level off someplace amenable to both parties. *In the meantime, it might be wiser to see the situation as it is and modify the expectations that were previously placed on our respective relationships. In doing so, we modify our relationships so that they have a better chance of withstanding the radical changes our babies bestow on our lives for better or worse.*

Identify and Recover What Is Still Viable from Your Former Self and Lifestyle

I wish someone had suggested this idea to me a long time ago. It's one that is typically overlooked. Under the strain of caring for the numerous needs of children, mothers often collapse physically, emotionally, mentally, and in all the other ways I've mentioned thus far. Their sense of self vanishes and with it all of the viable components that remain despite neglect or lack of attention. In my worst moments, I saw nothing but the dismal "facts" of my life as they were in that exact worst moment. I couldn't see or embrace the character traits that had always served me well in the past when my life hit a bump. I couldn't appreciate that I was an educated and talented individual. I couldn't access the energy to call the girlfriends who had been there during other trying moments of my life. All viable components of a life once lived, all viable components waiting to be retrieved on a moment's notice. When mothers are tired and worn out, they tend to forget all that they are, all that they have, and all that can be. On a good day, mothers must **take hold of what remains despite what changed when they became mothers.** They must think about the undertakings and projects that remain important to them; they must unearth the worthy personality traits that are buried beneath the dirty laundry and cynicism. They must recover what was valuable from their past so that they may enrich their future.

Regain Capacities Impaired by Stress

Stress generally impairs our ability to problem solve and cope effectively with the problems that emerge in our lives. To cope means to *actively* respond to the challenges that confront us. When we actively respond to the challenges that confront us, we typically (although not always consciously) identify the challenge, explore ways of dealing with the challenge, test our options, and act on the option that most successfully satisfies our objective before moving on to the next situation or problem that calls us to actively respond. It's a relatively straightforward approach that tends to falter quite dramatically when prolonged stress is placed in the equation. In fact, under stress many mothers actually magnify the problems they encounter, which further overwhelms them and renders them incapable of responding effectively. *In order to restore those capacities that are temporarily impaired by stress, mothers need to simplify their approach to coping by reducing the size of each challenge. That is, reduce each problem down to three steps: Identify, Decide, and Act.*

For example,
Identify: Don't get out with friends anymore
Decide: Set specific dates to see friends
Act: Make phone calls to friends AND babysitter

For example,
Identify: An unruly child
Decide: Find parenting class on how to discipline
Act: Attend parenting class and implement suggestions

For example,
Identify: Want to go back to school/work
Decide: When (now or later)
Act: Check budget and daycare options; enroll/return or plan for later

When I reduced my world of challenges down to these three steps, I felt empowered. The sensation of feeling empowered compelled me to further develop and hone my coping skills and problem-solving capacities. Over time and with practice, I faced each new challenge fully equipped with the variety of coping skills I had formerly used to manage my life. In the very best way, I resumed a life colored by the many shades of me. I redirected my life with each decision I made and every action I took, which led me closer to the sense of self I aspired to reclaim.

Recognize the Dissonance That Exists Between Life Before and After Children

I have found that asking the right questions can provide insight and understanding. In my quest to figure out why I was feeling so disjointed in my life as a mother, I looked to my past. Placing past and present side by side, questions came to mind that I knew had to be answered, for they illuminated the conflict that had become my experience. Consider the following questions.

"What was life like before you had children?"
Think about the activities that filled your days. Think about what you had come to *expect* of each day and the routines you engaged on a daily basis; that is, what was your schedule like? What did your days usually look like?

"What did you do prior to children that gave you a sense of satisfaction?"
Think about that flutter in your stomach and what put it there. If it wasn't a flutter, think about what put the big smile on your face or the strut in your stride. The activities may include things such as listening to good music, hiking, sharing a hearty laugh with friends, or participating in a sizzling debate among adversaries. You may have found satisfaction in a painting you never realized you could create or in the sweat you produced at the gym. It may have been taking on a particular project or completing one. Whatever it was, you knew it by the wave of delight you experienced after completing the activity.

"What were your hopes and dreams for the future apart from having children?"
I realize that most mothers feel compelled to mention children among their hopes and dreams for the future, but force yourself to think far enough back in time when the dream of children only materialized when you were sleeping. Rather, focus on those ambitions you expected to pursue regardless of children.

"When have you perceived yourself as living meaningfully?"
For some, living meaningfully might include reverence to God or a higher power. For others, it may be found in the paycheck that provides for a family or in the good deeds they perform throughout their community. The activities that have meaning in our lives may range from seemingly small tasks (making another person smile) to tasks that gain attention for their indisputable magnificence (charity work). Identify the times in your past when you were cognizant of living with

definite purpose. Remember what you saw, or maybe what you heard or felt during those moments.

"What achievements prior to children have been significant in your life?"
Was it learning a new skill or finishing a marathon? Was it earning a degree beyond your expectations or using your education to advance medicine or help a family out of crisis? An achievement may have come in the form of a realization or a personal success unbeknownst to others. After identifying those accomplishments, ask yourself *why* they were significant.

Once you've answered each of these questions, answer them again in the present tense. Chances are that you will find major differences between the two sets of answers; this is reasonable considering how priorities and responsibilities change radically once you have children. However, for many mothers, a big difference between the two sets of answers incites angst, conflicting feelings, and symptoms related to grief because in a heartbeat (no pun intended) their set of familiar expectations and perceptions were suddenly replaced with a set of unfamiliar expectations and perceptions. ***In other words, mothers may perceive change as loss, use negative self-talk, experience conflicting feelings, and slowly lose their sense of self when they perceive a substantial dissonance between how they achieved satisfaction, self-confidence, and self-esteem prior to motherhood and how they achieve it (or don't achieve it) after motherhood.*** For example, I attained a great sense of satisfaction, self-confidence, and self-esteem through graduate school and interacting with professors and colleagues. I am also aware that I achieved self-confidence and self-esteem by feeling attractive. I considered myself fit, pretty, pleasant, and somewhat charming, all of which seemed gone the day I raced to the hospital with my first labor pains. As I mentioned in an earlier chapter, I have plenty of pictures to prove my point. I sank fast and hard, losing all sense of my self that I had once taken for granted; I did not flourish as I had before. Understanding the contrast between how I once achieved meaning, satisfaction, and purpose before children and how I experienced them after children went a long way in helping me cope better and discover new ways of fulfilling the long-standing, long-forgotten, and decisive needs that once gave shape to my sense of self.

I devote the next and final chapter to the remaining goals of relearning the world and relearning your self. These two goals warrant an entire chapter since they are most crucial to the process of rediscovery. However, before moving on, I want to add a final note about the transition period and the various factors that affect how women adjust to this time in their lives. Generally speaking, each woman comes to motherhood with more or less well-developed coping skills, including how they coped with prior loss. Some women are simply better prepared emotionally and psychologically for the potential threat of losing their sense of self. Some women come into motherhood with a truly secure sense of self and a greater degree of self-confidence and self-esteem. Other women recognize the temporary state of adjustment and focus better on the here and now. By nature, there are women who can problem solve more effectively and adapt more quickly despite changing conditions. They know to reach out and find help when they need it, they talk about their feelings and limitations, and they take better care of themselves overall; that is, they maintain boundaries that protect their needs. They accept help without guilt and sustain, if not raise, their expectations of others to help them when they need it.

Finally, there are women who find the meaning and purpose in "family" quicker than other women and devote their energies in that direction without compromise. They discover meaningful answers to the questions that haunt others (e.g., "What happened to me?"), never even ask the questions, or tolerate not getting any answers to the questions they ask. Based on various life circumstances, personal histories, and general dispositions, women enter motherhood through one of countless doors, and their step into this new phase of life is wholly influenced by these factors. The good news is that a transitional period is just that. It's a shift in paradigm, a shift in perspective, a time that demands that women relearn the world and themselves. In relearning, mothers adjust and usually find their sense of self along with great satisfaction, joy, and purpose. However, it usually requires that mothers commit to the physical, emotional, and mental energy needed to relearn the world and themselves. I understand that these are precisely the energies depleted in the work associated with motherhood, which can further compromise one's capacity to cope. On the other hand, the decisions we make define the persons we become. And so, I encourage mothers to invest the energy (as depleted as it may be) needed to address the goals that might move them past grief and toward the relearning that may reestablish their self-confidence, self-esteem, and their overall sense of self.

EIGHT:
THROUGH THE EYES OF LOVE:
THE FINAL GOALS

o o o o o o o o o o o o o o o o o o o o o o o o o o o o o o o o o o o

The time will come
when, with elation,
you will greet yourself arriving
at your own door, in your own mirror,
and each will smile at the other's welcome,
and say, sit here. Eat.

You will love again the stranger who was your self.
Give wine, Give bread. Give back your heart
to itself, to the stranger who has loved you
all your life, whom you ignored
for another, who knows you by heart.
Take down the love letters from the bookshelf,
the photographs, the desperate notes, peel your own image from
the mirror.
Sit. Feast on your life.

—*Love After Love, by Derek Walcott, 1977*

Relearning the World

When I became a mother, many of my former ways of living life were disrupted. Prior to children, I had come to know the world in a certain way, a way I experienced first as a child, then as an adolescent, next as a single adult, and finally as a married adult. In all that time, I developed ways of thinking and behaving that reflected what I had collectively learned from living in the world. But on July 28, 1996, the world I had come to know changed, and I knew instantly that it would never be the same. It seemed only appropriate that I would have to relearn the world, a world with different routines, habits, companions, timetables, priorities, goals, expectations, and behaviors. Relearning the world is serious business that requires women to learn *how* to be themselves in a world changed by motherhood. This business extends far beyond a mere cognitive understanding *that* the world has changed with the presence of children.

When women become mothers they sense that the world is different, and that's because the world *is* different. When women become mothers they are also perceived differently by others, whether they continue to work outside the home or not. Conversely, mothers perceive others differently based on how others relate to their lives as parents. A great shift takes place that causes mothers to see the world out of a new lens. This new lens tends to focus on life events and all the different things (and people) that may enrich or jeopardize their children's interests, comfort, safety, and health. In one interview, a mother expressed how she became more conscious of environmental issues such as pollution and global warming since they were likely to impact her children as they grew up. Another mother voiced sheepishly how she thinks less like the Democrat she once was and more like the Conservative she remembers of her own mother. In another interview a mother described how she became more grounded in her faith, and another how she became involved in community activities that had never before held interest for her. Women become different when a baby is placed at the forefront of their lives, and the differences vary greatly. What's common among mothers is that they all relearn the world; relearning the world is a multifaceted process and a whole-person experience. That is, women relearn the world from an emotional, psychological, physical, social, and spiritual perspective wherein they appropriate new understanding of the world changed by the children who enter their lives. They develop a new posture, a new orientation in the world as mother, caregiver, teacher, role model, negotiator, provider, mediator, and disciplinarian.

Psychologically, I relearned the world in a way I never anticipated. The world seemed more threatening to me. Prior to children, I felt invincible and carefree. I had little to worry about and spent my days living frivolously. After children, I felt vulnerable in a way I had never felt before. I suppose I can equate this feeling to the adage "The more you have, the more you have to lose." Upon Leigh Ann's arrival, I experienced a love so deeply penetrating that I feared its loss instantly and quite profoundly. Worry became secondhand as I sat beside her in the NICU and worry followed me home a week later. I worried about her health, and mine. I worried about our bills, and our future. When life settled down and Leigh Ann moved well beyond threat, I started to worry about things that could happen to *me* that would jeopardize *her* happiness and that of my other children. I became acutely aware of all the things that could happen, all the things that could go terribly wrong. Worry in a world that can take away our joy in the blink of an eye. Emotionally, I expressed this worry in tears and in a greater awareness of time and the precious gift of having it. I became appreciative of the smallest things as my introspection grew. I embraced daily the blessings in my life and expressed my love generously, both physically and verbally, as I expanded my view of the world.

As mothers reorient themselves in the world, they also assess (often unwittingly) their physical and social environments. In their physical environment, they determine which objects, places, and conditions need to be avoided, discarded, or preserved. As one new (single) mother shared, "Bars are no longer an option." Several more mothers I interviewed declared their abstinence from drugs and other habits that they felt would somehow affect their children in a negative way. Similarly, in their social environment mothers choose family, friends, colleagues, business associates, and acquaintances in order of importance, and they relearn their relationships based on that order of importance. However harsh it may sound, life with a child is a busy life that can only accommodate a certain amount of activities, people, and priorities. Something usually has to give. Unfortunately, though, mothers tend to make decisions and choices that too frequently eliminate the physical and social elements that support their well-being because they aspire to *ideally* reorient themselves in a new world that has so many lofty, and tacit, expectations of them. For example, they may forgo trips to the gym in lieu of assuming the numerous chores at home. And they may abandon plans with friends in order to fulfill the ongoing list of obligations assumed to be theirs alone.

Nevertheless, as mothers move through this relearning phase, they incorporate a new perspective of the world as unique individuals embarking on a unique and unfolding experience given their distinct presuppositions, personal histories, temperaments, cultural backgrounds, and social status, all of which have a direct impact on how women adjust and learn to be themselves in a world rearranged by children. For instance, I'm sure that Julia Roberts and Gwyneth Paltrow relearned the world in a way unlike me and my friends based on their distinct perspective as movie stars, but we're similar in that we all formed a new integrity from interacting with a world broadened in scope and transformed by the children we love. *Relearning the world occurs naturally regardless of economic, marital, cultural, or social status.*

Relearning Your Self

Relearning your self may be the most difficult, albeit exhilarating, goal of all. This goal focuses entirely on how women relearn *themselves* once they transcend life without children and begin life with children. Once children are a part of their lives, women change; this fact is indisputable. Many things change as I emphasized in Chapter 1. However, a different (and necessary) kind of change transpires as women tackle the goal of reinterpreting their life stories and themselves in the unique and unfamiliar context of motherhood. The focal point of this relearning process involves women directing their energy toward discovering their limits and areas of vulnerability; adjusting to new patterns of caring and reexamining their most central beliefs, values, and convictions; re-creating their identity as well as revising their self-image. In addition, and central to MIA, the goal includes attention toward recovering self-esteem (and the self-confidence it conveys), which may have been shaken with the commencement of motherhood.

Luckily, we do not come into this world with a predetermined amount of self-confidence or self-esteem. They develop through our positive and negative interactions with others and the experiences we encounter. In particular, our self-confidence grows as we test and expand our capacities to function in relationship with others and through our achievements. As self-confidence builds over the course of years and our various perceptions take shape, we cultivate our sense of self. Our sense of self relies heavily on our degree of self-confidence, which is predominantly a measure of our self-worth. Self-worth is just another way of describing self-esteem.

Self-esteem is the foundation on which we structure our sense of self. It is a fundamental component in our ability to experience true satisfaction. In all that we do, we can't truly appreciate the good unless we possess a certain degree of self-esteem. It's our self-esteem that "tells" us that we've done well, and we, in turn, feel good about ourselves. Self-esteem is ultimately how we think about ourselves; however, it is not always how we really are. People with high self-esteem tend to capitalize on the positive images they've created *for* themselves *about* themselves; they internalize those positive images. They are generally happier, more energetic, and more confident in their endeavors because of these positive images.

On the other hand, people with low self-esteem tend to internalize negative images; they often battle depression and other debilitating maladies. However, the task of building self-esteem can be as easy as creating more positive images of oneself, which then promotes more constructive internal dialogue and behavior. The reciprocal nature of this task makes for a remarkable effect; that is, as self-esteem becomes greater, the images become more positive, thus creating higher self-esteem, which again becomes evident in our words and actions. I realize this sounds too easy, almost ridiculous, but it actually works when practiced with diligence and precision. And it works by simply *thinking* about the images to which we aspire.

Altering Negative Self-Images Using NLP

The images that we retain in our mind's eye can fall anywhere between incredibly positive and horribly negative. Our horrible images are usually severe, exaggerated, and very negative in content. The trick is to literally reduce or shrink the negative images in size (i.e., form) and replace them with images that are grand in form and positive in content. This technique is used extensively in Neuro-Linguistic Programming (NLP), a study of human behavior that emphasizes the connection between how we use verbal and nonverbal language (words, phrases, gestures, and habits) to reveal what we think and believe given the information we perceive through seeing, hearing, tasting, feeling, and smelling. In using the term "programming," this technology proposes that our thoughts, feelings, and actions can become habitual but may be changed by switching or "upgrading" our mental software. Because NLP presupposes that specific thoughts, feelings, and actions combine to create a specific experience or result, we can eliminate an unwanted result or experience by changing our thoughts, feelings, and actions. Below is an NLP exercise aimed at changing a negative self-image.

NLP Exercise

1. Close your eyes and think of an image you have of yourself, any image. Look closely at the picture and determine if it's large or small in size (form).

2. Look at the content. Determine if it's negative or positive. If it's negative, check for any physical distortions in the image; that is, see the picture of yourself as you really are.

3. Modify the negative content. Think of a more positive aspect of the image you have represented in your mind's eye. For example, if you see

yourself as angry and the meaning you derive from that image is that you are awful to be with, realize that anger is an ally intending to help you; anger signals distress. It's a legitimate emotion that must be addressed; it is not who you are. Change the image to reflect this understanding. Create a new image with positive content—an image that accentuates your strengths, your favorite personality traits, your greatest abilities. Be as specific as you can. Being very specific works to your advantage.

4. Take this new image and make it big and bright. Zoom in so you can see it closely. Add color or make it 3-D. Turn it into a movie if you like.

5. Repeat this exercise until it becomes automatic, so that it appears when you want or need it to appear.

As Earl Nightingale said, "We become what we think about." So think good thoughts. Consciously choose to change negative thoughts and how you represent those thoughts. With the ability to change your images, your internal representations, you empower your self-esteem, and consequently your emotions and behaviors.

Altering Negative Internal Dialogue Using NLP

Besides negative self-images, mothers often have negative internal dialogues (the things they tell themselves). Using negative internal language destroys confidence, minimizes self-esteem, and undermines positive intentions. I remember being hard on myself when I first became a mother. My mantra, my inner voice, would say, "What's the matter with you?" or "You can't do this. This is too hard." Throughout the years, the voice continued to ask, "What's wrong with you?" and "Why can't you do this? Other mothers do it and they make it look easy." I would have these thoughts especially after a bad moment like a fit of rage over something trivial. Worse still was that I started to *believe* that things would *never* get better. I was stuck in all kinds of negativity, and I was becoming more depressed and desperate for change. I think it may have been my husband who recalled for me the NLP skills I once possessed. So, with nothing to lose, I brushed off the dusty NLP skills and had a little fun using a technique aimed at altering a negative internal voice by simply changing its tonality. For instance, I made my inner voice sound like Donald Duck, with a lisp that could bring a smile to anyone's face. I even gave Donald a southern drawl when I needed a good laugh. This exercise was powerful in disarming "the charge" I originally gave my inner voice, but it did not elicit the positive intention that NLP seeks.

An NLP presupposition is that "underlying every behavior is a positive intention," which means that *my negative internal voice was actually trying to do something positive for me.* As skeptical as I can be at times, I figured that I might as well give it a try. The intention spoke without reservation when I asked, "What are you trying to do for me?" In a kind, slow, and deliberate voice I heard, "Save you." I remember crying and feeling for the first time that I would be all right. I instantly became less critical of myself, knowing that "the critic" was actually on my side. I may not have liked the tone in which it spoke or the words it chose, but I did appreciate its intention. The critical voice was intending to shake me up and make me take notice of other mothers who seemed happy and in control of the chaotic life that had bewildered me. What were they doing that I wasn't? I had things to learn, and they would teach me. The voice was also trying to point out how my general personality was not suited to a lifestyle that catered to children all day, every day, without help. The voice was reminding me of my need for space, quiet, and relief. It was helpful for me to weed out the positive intention concealed within my negative internal dialogue and agree with that intention; in doing so, I neutralized the internal voice that was crippling the self-esteem that I needed to reclaim the sense of self that I craved. Once I neutralized the negative tone and content of my inner voice, I began rebuilding my self-esteem with affirming self-talk.

Reframing

Affirming self-talk incapacitates negative internal dialogue, including the dialogue that incorporates statements that would have you believing in words such as "never," "everybody," "always," and "no one." Words such as these are considered overgeneralizations. While they beg the question, "Really?" they sabotage self-esteem. Fortunately, affirming self-talk reframes overgeneralizations by presenting the otherwise negative statements as positive assertions. For instance, take the simple sentence, "No one understands." I heard several mothers say these three words as though they were fact. The truth is, they aren't fact. I shook my head empathically as if to agree, and responded, "Really? No one? Of all the people you know, of all the people you relate to on a daily basis, there is not *one* person you believe would understand what you are going through?" Each and every mother answered the same way. "Well, okay. I suppose I know some other moms who would understand." Of course there are other mothers who understand.

There may be a few "always," "never," and "no one" realities that exist, but this is certainly not one of them.

A reframing of "No one understands" could be, "I feel lonely in my experience, but I have friends/acquaintances/family I can turn to for understanding and support." Usually, negative internal dialogues target self-esteem more directly by disparaging comments such as "You're a terrible mom" or "You can't even discipline your kids right." In taking affirmative action and reframing this kind of negative internal dialogue, one might try something more like, "You're a good mom having a bad day. It happens." Or, in the second example you might try, "Some kids can be difficult to discipline. Try a different approach to get the results you want." As I mentioned in Chapter 5, "The Ripple Effect," *you can choose to change.* All it takes is effort and the conviction that it works. Choose to change your negative internal dialogue by using the simple method of reframing. By reframing, you're likely to experience an *immediate* difference in how you feel and act.

> *"Human beings, by changing the inner attitudes of their minds, can change the outer aspects of their lives."*
>
> —William James

Affirmations

Internal dialogues generate images, and those images may be negative or positive depending on your prompts. Articulate your thoughts in the negative and you convey messages that adversely affect your emotions and thwart your sense of self. Articulate your thoughts in the positive and you preserve a greater degree of your self-confidence and self-esteem. With the added use of one-sentence affirmations such as those suggested by renowned motivational speakers and writers, you may rejuvenate your spirit, embrace possibilities, and turn your life in the direction you prefer. My best friend Danya gave me a book three years ago for my birthday, a book that encouraged me to write affirmations that supported my creativity and ability to write. I wrote the following affirmations daily:

I have important things to say.
I am willing to create.
I am genuinely talented.
I am very creative.
I can do this.
Expect the universe to support your dream. It will.

The affirmations you choose should not contradict how you actually perceive yourself. If they do, you could very well hear a second inner voice that sounds sarcastic or skeptical. When this occurs, the affirmations are not likely to work; therefore, rewrite the affirmations by stating the intention of *learning* what you desire. For instance, "I am learning how to love myself" or "I am learning how to be patient." Your affirmations will then be congruent with your perceptions, and you will obtain greater success. In the stillness of your life, you will recognize if your affirmations are having the effect you intend. If they're not, you might explore what positive intention exists behind the sarcastic or skeptical voice that persists (as discussed earlier). Finally, you could practice seeing yourself through someone else's eyes. When you can see yourself objectively through the eyes of someone who you know loves you, you gain a perspective unlike your own, which may ultimately help you acknowledge and honor your intrinsic worth.

How Family and Friends Can Help

Self-affirming internal dialogues, affirmations, techniques that enhance self-worth, and restructuring a self-image can help a "lost" mother realize the goal of relearning her self in a new world spawned by children. In relearning her self, each woman assumes a highly idiosyncratic challenge that demands that she invest a certain degree of energy in her own resurgence, in her ultimate goal of reclaiming a sense of self transformed by the uneasiness of change. For instance, a spouse cannot change your perspective or derive meaning in your life. A sister cannot rebuild your self-esteem or modify your behaviors, motivations, habits, and priorities. A best friend cannot change the way you interact with others or enforce your boundaries. And your mother, as much as she may want to, cannot change your negative internal dialogue or give you the energy you need to endure and cope with the stress related to your transition. However, family and friends can do many other things to be supportive in your time of need, things you may suggest to them if they are not already doing them. They include the following:

- reassure you that you need not take on every task at once
- normalize your feelings
- encourage you to pace yourself
- listen empathically; encourage emotional expressions
- comfort you in your worst moments

- help you recognize your strengths and limitations in coping
- tolerate your feelings without judgment
- respect your strong and weaker boundaries
- encourage you to pursue former goals and important projects
- help you discover new goals and aspirations
- discourage selfishness in others
- help you determine your triggers
- give you time to "escape," rest, and refresh
- identify options you cannot see
- gather information and resources that support your needs
- encourage counseling if appropriate
- appreciate the enormity of your "job"
- appreciate how motherhood affects the different aspects of your life
- appreciate your attempts to reclaim your lost sense of self

Family and friends can take an active role in supporting you, but they cannot do for you what you must do for yourself. In taking an active role in relearning your self, you accept the opportunity to establish your values and incorporate boundaries that are necessary to protect those values. In taking an active role in relearning your self, you step out of helplessness and into changing aspects of your thoughts, feelings, and actions that will affect you and your life in many positive ways. In taking an active role in relearning your self, you declare that you are not choiceless; you accept the challenge to engage the goals that lead to a renewed sense of self, and you act to reclaim the sense of self you lost while functioning in your role as mother. I agree with Oprah Winfrey that motherhood *is* the hardest job in the world; mothers are responsible for the development, nurturance, and well-being of another human being. When a job involves this depth of attention, caring, giving, and sacrificing for another on a daily basis, dark and desperate moments can occur for a weary caregiver. It's reasonable and understandable.

Conclusion

Within these pages I've exposed some of my worst moments, moments and feelings that were easier to write than to say aloud to family and friends at the time I was actually having those bad moments. I know firsthand how difficult it can be to confess to the seemingly horrid feelings and thoughts that can accompany the trying times of mothering one's child. However, all my moments, all my feelings and thoughts, have created the mother and woman I am today. I hope I have adequately expressed what I have learned from my experience and from the experiences of other mothers. Apart from learning about the path grief takes when mothers perceive loss in their lives, I have learned how mothers generally "reconcile" with those losses. *The one thing I know for sure is that reconciling with loss begins with acknowledging its existence. Once mothers recognize and acknowledge the changes in their lives that register emotionally as losses, they can begin to deal with their grief in the most productive manner.*

The grief work embedded within the goals I outlined earlier acts as a means of reconciling with the changes mothers often experience and equate with loss. In addressing these goals, mothers challenge themselves to grow in spite of the temporary or permanent losses they perceive. In general, grief work entails relearning the world and ourselves within the world. Grief work inspires new patterns of living that include new habits, new awareness, and a new sense of being without the people, places, and things that we have lost. While working through grief, we establish a new integrity and new ways of thriving despite the ache that remains. Although it's rarely an easy time, it *is* a time that allows for growth should we accept the challenge to experience wholeness in a way unlike what we knew before loss. With this understanding, women who become mothers are challenged to develop give-and-take relationships within a new and larger whole called family. Within that family, they adjust to a new purpose, a new meaning, and a world full of new experiences; however, this must not deny their need for a strong and well-rounded sense of self that flourishes apart from and beyond their role of mother.

When a mother maintains a healthy sense of self, she functions every day with all the possibilities and potential to live fully as herself and to relate to others in the most satisfying ways. Anything short of this over a prolonged period of time may create symptoms consistent with grief as viewed in the context of grief as anxiety, or Maternal Intrapersonal Anxiety (MIA). *Ultimately, MIA results when the values central in a woman's life are consistently denied, suppressed, ignored, or violated because it's those specific values that anchor her sense of self.* To maintain a strong sense of self, women must continue to utilize the strategies that worked to restore what they lost in the first place. It requires that they stay actively invested in their physical, emotional, and mental care, which includes accepting help that others (family, friends, neighbors, and acquaintances) can and are willing to provide. It also means staying attuned to the values most central in their lives and protecting those values with appropriate boundaries. Enforcing appropriate boundaries builds the confidence and self-esteem that allows a sense of self to thrive unconditionally. With a healthy sense of self intact, mothers will no longer be missing in action (or experiencing MIA), but rather taking action to be fully themselves in a new world, with new purpose, and with a renewed sense of self that incorporates all that is important to them, a sense of self that confidently claims, "I know who I am."

A TRIBUTE

"The loving mother teaches her child to walk alone. She is far enough from him so that she cannot actually support him, but she holds out her arms to him. She imitates his movements, and if he totters, she swiftly bends as if to seize him, so that the child might believe he is not walking alone.... And yet, she does more. Her face beckons like a reward, an encouragement. Thus, the child walks alone with his eyes fixed on his mother's face, **not** *on the difficulties in his way. He supports himself by the arms that do not hold him, and constantly strives towards the refuge in his mother's embrace, little suspecting* **that in the very same moment that he is emphasizing his need of her, he is proving that he can do without her,** *because he is walking alone."*

—Soren Kierkegaard

Thank you for all that you do and all that you are in the lives of your children. My sincere best wishes in your quest to renew your sense of self.

—Anne M. Smollon

REFERENCES

Attig, T., (1996). *How We Grieve: Relearning the World*. New York, NY: Oxford University Press.

Andreas, S., and Faulkner, C. (eds.). (1994). *NLP: The New Technology Of Achievement*. New York, NY: HarperCollins Publishers.

Crittenden, A. (2001). *The Price of Motherhood: Why the Most Important Job in the World Is Still the Least Valued*. New York, NY: Henry Holt and Company.

Mitchell, K. R., and Anderson, H. (1983). *All Our Losses, All Our Griefs: Resources for Pastoral Care*. Philadelphia, PA: The Westminster Press.

Sanders, C. M., (1992). *Surviving Grief ... And Learning To Live Again*. New York, NY: John Wiley & Sons, Inc.

Sullender, R. S. (1985). *Grief and Growth: Pastoral Resources for Emotional and Spiritual Growth*. Mahwah, NY: Paulist Press.

Switzer, D. K., (1970). *The Dynamics Of Grief: Its Source, Pain, and Healing*. Nashville, TN: Abingdon Press.

Viorst, J. (1986). *Necessary Losses*. New York, NY: Ballantine Books.

Whitfield, C. L., (1993). *Boundaries And Relationships: Knowing, Protecting, and Enjoying the Self*. Deerfield Beach, FL: Health Communications, Inc.

978-0-595-41324-9
0-595-41324-2

Printed in the United States
87791LV00003B/385-411/A